Workshop on Empirical Translation Process Research

Held at AMTA 2022

Orlando, Florida, USA
12-16 September 2022

ISBN: 978-1-7138-6760-9

Printed from e-media with permission by:

Curran Associates, Inc.
57 Morehouse Lane
Red Hook, NY 12571

Printed with permission by Curran Associates, Inc. (2023)

For permission requests, please contact the Association for Computational Linguistics at the address below.

Association for Computational Linguistics
209 N. Eighth Street
Stroudsburg, Pennsylvania 18360

Phone: 1-570-476-8006
Fax: 1-570-476-0860

acl@aclweb.org

Additional copies of this publication are available from:

Curran Associates, Inc.
57 Morehouse Lane
Red Hook, NY 12571 USA
Phone: 845-758-0400
Fax: 845-758-2633
Email: curran@proceedings.com
Web: www.proceedings.com

AMTA ORLANDO 2022

The 15th Conference of the Association for Machine Translation in the Americas

2022.amtaweb.org

PROCEEDINGS

Workshop on Empirical Translation Process Research

Organizer: Michael Carl

Introduction: Workshop on Empirical Translation Process Research

Michael Carl mcarl6@kent.edu
Kent State University, Ohio, USA

Masaru Yamada yamada@apple-eye.com
Rikkyo University, Tokyo, Japan

Longhui Zou lzou4@kent.edu
Kent State University, Ohio, USA

1 Empirical Translation Process Research

Empirical Translation Process Research (TPR) investigates human translation and post-editing processes. Starting with introspective methods, i.e., transcribed Think-Aloud Protocols (TAP) and intro/retrospective reports, TPR has since the 1980s evolved in several stages with the increasing availability and usage of new sensor and recording technologies. Keylogging has been used since the mid-1990s to assess translation effort (temporal, technical, cognitive) and translation effects (e.g., translation quality, productivity) and eyetracking technology has been introduced in TPR around 10 years later. Together, keylogging and eyetracking technology have been used to illuminate the relation between the input (gazing patterns) and output (typing behavior) of the translators' black box, sometimes complemented by translators' introspection and self-reports, and to a lesser extent also brain imaging methods (EEG, fMRI, fNIRS). The main aim has been to determine "what goes on in the head of translators", how we can conceptualize and measure the assumed translation processes and how those processes relate to / vary with respect to different textual features (e.g., metaphors, terminology, easy, vs. difficult syntax), different types of text (technical, news, literature, etc.), expertise of translators (e.g., novice vs. experienced translators), different translation purpose (e.g., informative translation, light vs. full post-editing), usage of translation technology (CAT, MT post-editing, external search, etc.), and to what extent different target languages correlate with different translation patterns. Recently, the scope of TPR has also included spoken language production (including translation dictation, sight translation, interpretation, sight interpretation, etc.), subtitling and audio-visual translation, fan-subbing, re-speaking, and other forms of translation production.

2 Ecological Validity in TPR

Ecological Validity — i.e., the importance of TPR for the "real world" context — has sometimes been questioned. While most translators work with commercial translation tools (such as Trados or memoQ), much of TPR has been conducted in more artificial environments, such as Translog-II. However, since recently there is a possibility to convert Trados Studio keylogging data (collected via Qualitivity) into Translog-II format and to add the converted data to the CRITT TPR-DB. The newly devised *Trados-to-Translog* tool synchronizes with the output of various eye-trackers (currently Tobii, Eyelink, and GazePoint). This allows us to investigate user activity data collected during translation sessions in Trados as a combination of eye movement and keyboard logging. It provides thereby the possibility to record translation behavior in an ecologically realistic translation environment. We are now able to explore patterns of reading and typing activities in a widely and professionally used CAT tool, and thus to achieve a better understanding of factors that impact professional translation activity.

3 WeTPR

The Workshop on Empirical Translation Process Research (WeTPR) aims at fostering empirical TPR, to document the current state of the art in TPR, to point to promising research avenues, innovative research questions and research methods, and reporting new measures and findings, to disseminate TPR results and broaden awareness of TPR among the MT community.

We have invited **Karl Friston** to talk about *The graphical brain and deep inference* and we have gathered seven additional contributions that address topics within the field of TPR, including technical, practical, and theoretical papers, conceptual statements and empirical de-scriptions of experiments and experiences that address TPR from a computational, linguistic, psychological, cognitive, or philosophical point of view. In light of this, WeTPR provides a forum to discuss up-to-date developments in TPR.

4 The Future of TPR

We anticipate that empirical TPR will make two significant c ontributions. First, empirical TPR will contribute to the improvement of translation practices. Findings from empirical TPR will make predictions about translation difficulty, w h ich l e ads t o p o ssible e x planations f o r more frequently occurred translation errors. TPR findings m ay a lso p rovide i nsights i nto translator training. As the value of human translation is often neglected with increased quality of machine translation, TPR can provide evidence for the significance of the translators and their future role in the translation industry. From this perspective, the increasing ecological validity of TPR is a meaningful step forward.

Another contribution of TPR is the demystification o f h u man l a nguage a n d translation. 20th-century linguistics has tried to answer this questions assuming translation is an interlingual process transforming thought across languages into surface word forms. Noam Chomsky, for instance, postulated a *transformational* grammar that is instantiated in our brains, to map deep logical structures into words. In contrast TPR is a bottom-up approach attempting to unravel translation processes based on empirical data. It thereby draws on recent academic disciplines including neuro- and computer science that aim at elucidating mental processes in terms of probabilistic input-output and encoder-decoder based transformation processes. Through this interdisciplinary investigation, empirical TPR strives to demystify human language, translation and multilingualism in general.

5 Program Committee

- Adolfo M. García, Universidade de SanAndrés, Argentina
- Ali Saeedi, Kent State University, USA
- Álvaro Marín García, University of Valladolid, Spain
- Arianna Bisazza, University of Groningen, Netherlands
- Christian Olalla Soler, University of Bologna, Italy
- Cristina Toledo Báez, University of Málaga, Spain
- David Orrego-Carmona, Aston University, UK

- Defeng Li, University of Macau, Macau
- Devin Gilbert, Utah Valley University, USA
- Fabio Alves, Federal University of Minas Gerais, Brazil
- Félix do Carmo, University of Surrey, UK
- Feng Jia, Renmin University of China, China
- Haruka Ogawa, Earlham College, USA
- Igor AL da Silva, Universidade Federal de Uberlândia, Brazil
- Jean Nitzke, Johannes Gutenberg University of Mainz, Germany
- Jiajun Qian, Shanghai Maritime University, China
- Jun PAN, Hong Kong Baptist University, Hong Kong
- Kristian Tangsgaard Hvelplund, University of Copenhagen, Denmark
- Maarit Koponen, University of Eastern Finland, Finland
- Miguel Jiménez, Rutgers University, USA
- Natália Resende, Dublin City University, Ireland
- Ricardo Muñoz Martín, University of Bologna, Italy
- Sheila Castilho, Dublin City University, Ireland
- Sanjun Sun, Beijing Foreign Studies University, China
- Yuxiang Wei, Kent State University, USA

Contents

The graphical brain and deep inference

Karl Friston

Abstract: This presentation considers deep temporal models in the brain. It builds on previous formulations of active inference to simulate behaviour and electrophysiological responses under deep (hierarchical) generative models of discrete state transitions. The deeply structured temporal aspect of these models means that evidence is accumulated over distinct temporal scales, enabling inferences about narratives (i.e., temporal scenes). We illustrate this behaviour in terms of Bayesian belief updating – and associated neuronal processes – to reproduce the epistemic foraging seen in reading. These simulations reproduce these sort of perisaccadic delay period activity and local field potentials seen empirically; including evidence accumulation and place cell activity. These simulations are presented as an example of how to use basic principles to constrain our understanding of system architectures in the brain – and the functional imperatives that may apply to neuronal networks.

Differentiated Measurements for Fatigue and Demotivation in Translation Process

Junyi Mao sczs16@durham.ac.uk
Durham University, Durham, UK

Abstract

Fatigue is physical and mental weariness caused by prolonged continuity of work and would undermine work performance. In translation studies, although fatigue is a confounding factor previous experiments all try to control, its detection and measurement are largely ignored. To bridge this lacuna, this article recommends some subjective and objective approaches to measuring translation fatigue based on prior fatigue research. Meanwhile, as demotivation is believed to be an emotion that confounds its accurate measurements, a discussion on how to distinguish those two states is further conducted from theoretical and methodological perspectives. In doing so, this paper not only illuminates on how to measure two essential influencers of translation performance, but also offers some insights into the distinction of affective and physical states during translation process.

1 Introduction

With the flourish of experimental studies on translation process, translators' cognitive and affective states at workplaces have gained increasing attention. However, compared with intense probes into the cognitive aspect of translation, how translators' emotional states influence their translation performance remains largely underexplored. And one of essential reasons is the shortage of reliable instruments to record interested variables accurately and concurrently, especially when the ecological validity is considered. Even though, recent decades have witnessed a growing number of endeavours on translators' emotion (Kitanovska-Kimovska & Cvetkoski, 2022; Lehr, 2014; Lehr & Hvelplund, 2020; Rojo & Caro, 2016), stress (details in Weng & Zheng, 2020) in particular, and motivation (Fan, 2012; Ghasem, 2019; Wu, 2019). Of note is that most experiments adopted subjective measurements (e.g., emotional or motivation scales) to investigate translators' affective states, which somehow ignores the inevitable discrepancy between self-evaluation and actual moods. In this regard, Weng and Zheng's (2020) combination of State-Trait Anxiety Inventory and biomarkers such as heart rate, blood pressure, skin conductance, and salivary cortisol is methodologically progressive. As there exist overlaps between biometrics used to measure different emotional and/or physical states, scholars have advocated the proper application of those techniques and meticulous interpretation of relevant data (Richter & Slade, 2017; Rojo & Korpal, 2020). In translation studies, Rojo and Korpal (2020) have elaborated on how to distinguish stress from other emotions when heart rate variability and skin conductance are employed as indicators. According to their review, no compelling evidence exists to support the assumption that discrete categories of emotions uniquely correspond to specific region(s) of brain, and the same applies to other biomarkers. Thus, the multiple explanations of same physiological indices are an obstacle to overcome before those cutting-edged devices are fully capitalised on. The story grows complexity when physical, cognitive, and emotional factors share one same indicator, of which pupil dilation is an example. Though researchers have designed experiments conscientiously to eliminate common confounding variables such as fatigue, to what extent such manipulations are successful remains unknown. As fatigue is a universally concerned influencer in translation experiments, this article proposes some measurements for translation fatigue with reference to previous literature on fatigue theories and measurements. Afterwards, a comparison between demotivation and fatigue is conducted from the perspective of conceptualisation and measurement. In doing so, it suggests on how to distinguish two phenomenologically similar states in translation scenarios and offers some methodological insights into differentiating physical states from affective states.

2 Fatigue

2.1 Theoretical Definition of Fatigue

State fatigue is defined as "weariness or exhaustion from labour, exertion, or stress" in Merriam Webster dictionary, which denotes its physical and mental aspects. Theoretically speaking, fatigue can also function as a trait since certain people have stronger propensity to feel exhausted under the same workload. Comparatively, physical fatigue gains less theoretical interest than mental fatigue, for which diverse frameworks have been proposed. At first, mental fatigue is depicted as a psychobiological state caused by lengthy and uninterrupted periods of attention-demanding tasks and features a feeling of energy-depletion (Boksem & Tops, 2008). And its adverse impacts on cognitive and motor performances are believed to originate from an impairment in attention maintenance (Boksem et al., 2005), self- regulation (Lorist et al., 2005), response promptness and accuracy (Boksem et al., 2006), as well as efficiency of information identification and utilisation (Lorist et al., 2000). As its conception evolves, more emphasis was placed on its indication of inefficient energy management. According to Thorndike (1900), fatigue is indexed by the inability to do the right thing, rather than continue to work over sustained time. Likewise, Bartley and Chute (1947) believe the conflict between competing behavioural dispositions as the essence of fatigue. By this logic, fatigue is an adaptive state serving to maintain effective and systematic management of goals and meanwhile signifying one's motivational control (details in Balkin & Wesensten, 2011). Also, theoretical attention has been paid to what determine the occurrence of mental fatigue. On a macro level, Grandjean (1968) posited that contextual elements, internal physical factors, and task features altogether accelerate the accumulation of fatigue, which can be alleviated by off-task or leisure activities. In comparison, microcosmic models explain cognitive fatigue through the lens of attention availability and utilisation. For instance, Kahneman's (1973) model on attention allocation delineates the prerequisites for a task to be fatiguing. It postulates that individuals' overall arousal during a task depends on the attentional resources available, whose distribution is a combined effect of one's long-term task interest, state motivation, and regular evaluations on the goal-performance discrepancy. To modify Kahneman's model, Hockey (1997) further included competence-related factors such as responses to challenges, capacity for sustained work, and tolerance of stress as well as perception-related element of task value (Hockey, 1997:80). In his viewpoint, when demands exceed efforts budgeted for the task, a downward revision of goals might be adopted to alleviate the discrepancy until a complete disengagement take places. Similarly, the integrated resource allocation model (Kanfer & Ackerman, 1989) surmised that the quantity of attention accessible for allocation is a joint function of one's ability and willingness. Attention can be diverted to task effort, off- task thoughts and distractions, and self-regulation. And it is the self-perception of effort-performance, performance-utility, and effort-utility functions that determines how much attention one would commit to the given task (details in Ackerman, 2011:21-23). Taken together, those theories not only explicate the role of personal characteristics, time on task, and task features in determining the fatigue effect (Kanfer, 2011:197-198), but also imply the interwoven relationship between motivation and fatigue in conditioning energy distribution and goal setting. It is such a functional overlap between demotivation and fatigue that legitimates the inclusion of motivational factors in some well-recognised fatigue scales (e.g.,Ahsberg's Occupational Fatigue Inventory).

In practice, apart from measurements of fatigue targeting clinic populations, various self-report and observational indicators for chronic and state fatigues have been developed and implemented in cognitive and physical tasks. The following part introduces typical measurements of fatigue for healthy people and examines their applicability in translation studies.

2.2 Measurement of Fatigue

Subjective Measurement of Fatigue

For nonclinical populations, subjective measurements of fatigue consist of task-specific scales, general scales, and measures of related constructions (details in Ackerman, 2011:24). The first type focuses on one single dimension of subjective fatigue (e.g., Stress-state measures in Matthews & Desmond, 2002). The second kind is more diversified with a distinction between short-term and long-term fatigue (e.g., Occupational Fatigue Inventory; Åhsberg, 2000) as well as trait (e.g., Modified Fatigue Impact Scale; Larson, 2013; Fatigue Severity Scale; Krupp, 1989) and state fatigue (e.g., Visual Analog Scale of Fatigue; Lee et al., 1991). Most of those inventories incorporate physical, psychosocial, and cognitive aspects of fatigue and measure the fatigue intensity on a Likert-based scale. In the last case, fatigue is assessed as a component of its highly relevant variables ranging from the activity level (Brooket et al., 1979), moods (Mcnair et al., 1971), activation–deactivation (Thayer, 1978), to tiredness (Montgomery, 1983). When implemented, different scales are often combined, and a comparison of pre-task and post-task data reveals the fatigue caused by a lengthy and attention-demanding task. For instance, when Trejo et al. (2005) examined cognitive fatigue in a continuous mental arithmetic task, both Activation Deactivation Adjective Checklist and Visual Analogue Mood Scale were administered. As evidence on individualised influences (e.g., personality) over self-rated fatigue accrues, meticulous scholars began to enclose personality tests into their instruments. A case in point is Ackerman and Kanfer's (2009) investigation on how the temporal length of SAT test impacts self-rated cognitive fatigue, which shows that differences in neuroticism accounted for the variance in pre-test and post-test cognitive fatigue. However inclusive current fatigue scales are, subjective data is criticised for being unidentical to real-time states, not to mention the concurrent influence of individual differences. In this sense, objective measurements serve as a healthy supplement.

Objective Measurement of Fatigue

Performance as a Fatigue Indicator: Although a decrement in performance after a long-period task execution is accepted as one objective marker of fatigue (Hockey, 2011:171), the validity of such a proposition depends on the satisfaction of following requirements: 1). for a between-group comparison, participants' task specific competency and differences in fatigue proneness and regulation should be considered as confounding factors; for a within-subject comparison, task difficulty should be controlled at a comparable level. 2). time-on-task is key to distinguishing fatigue effects from those of others (e.g., unfamiliarity with experimental setting-up) when task difficulty is within one's competency. Fatigue normally occurs at the later stage of a lengthy and continuous task, which means underperformance at the onset is nonattributable to fatigue unless a taxing task is deliberately assigned beforehand. 3). the task must be intrinsically enjoyable and attention-demanding so that confounders of amotivation or boredom can be eliminated. Even though, extensive evidence has shown that direct effects of fatigue on task performance can be unnoticeable (Ackerman, 2011:14-15), which according to Compensatory Control Model (Hockey, 1997), may result from self-regulation and cognitive control. From this perspective, performance may not be an effective and reliable index of translation fatigue as self-reports and physiological markers do.

Physiological Markers as Fatigue Indicators: Prior experiments resorting to biomarkers cover varied cognitive and physical tasks, among which literature on drivers' fatigue has established a systematic measurement mechanism. In Ani et al.'s (2020) review of detecting systems for driving fatigue, extant approaches were summarised as behavioural, physiological, psychophysical, and biomechanical based. As to behaviours observable by naked eyes, yawning, eye closure or blinking, and changed head or sitting positions can manifest the appearance of fatigue. To capture more subtle changes of physiological signals precisely, electrocardiogram (ECG), electromyogram (EMG), electrooculogram (EOG), electroencephalogram (EEG) and eye trackers have been applied. As far as ecological validity and operational simplicity is concerned, eye trackers seemingly outperform neuro-imaging detectors. And eye-related indicators in service range from eye closure, blink, saccades, fixation, to pupil dilation. Of note is that most research co-used different indices to represent the multi-facets of fatigue. Considering translators' normal work environments, indices of practical value are enumerated in Table1 along with cautions on their application.

Fatigue type	Author & task situation	Tools	Variables and signs of fatigue	Measurement and data analysis, findings	Applicability in translation
Muscular fatigue	Rahayu *et al*, 2016 Driving test	Grip pressure measurement System	Decrease in hand grip pressure force	Compare the force of hands during the first and the last 15-min sessions	Applicable
		EMG	Higher average EMG responses indicates higher level of fatigue	Electrodes were put on the skin surface of interested muscles, and compare data from the first and the last 15-min sessions	Applicable
	Zhang *et al*, 2014 2-hour driving simulation	EMG	Lower tonus of EMG signals increased fatigue	Electrodes were put on the subjects' neck and occiput	Applicable
Muscular visual fatigue		EOG	Decreased eye movement and increased blink rate signal fatigue	Electrodes were placed on the upper eyelid	Applicable
Cognitive/ mental fatigue	Jing *et al*., 2020 Field driving	portable EEG cap	increase in α & β frequency band and a decrease in β frequency band	$(\alpha+\theta)/\beta$ positively relates to self-rated fatigue; $(\alpha+\theta)/\beta$ negatively relates to self-rated fatigue	Applicable
	Zhang *et al*., 2014	EEG	Self-developed algorithm	Electrodes were placed on O1 and O2	Data analysis is too complicated
	Punsawad *et al*., 2015 Simulated driving	electrode cap with Ag/AgCl electrodes & EEG amplifier	three different weighting factors applied to the index $(\theta+\alpha)/\beta$	Electrodes placed in opposition to dominant hand on Temporal, Central, and Parietal areas.	
	Antons *et al*., 2012 Listen to 40-min audios of different qualities for comprehensi-on tasks	EEG (Ag/AgCl electrodes)	An increase in Theta and Alpha frequencies	Electrodes were placed on 7 standard locations with a reference electrode on the tip of the nose. filter data with the threshold of 40 Hz and used data from electrodes with the highest band in the first and last 10-min	Applicable
	Peng *et al*., 2022 vigilance test, cognitive task (foreign language reading and math), or simulated driving	Wearable functional near infrared spectroscopy (fMRI)	functional connectivity strength, characteristics of brain functional network, and time-domain characteristics of blood oxygen	From no to moderate fatigue, the network connectivity overall decreased, especially between regions of PFC and FEF, PFC and PMC. From moderate to severe fatigue, the network connectivity overall increased, and a relatively compact connectivity remained between left PFC and other regions, especially between PFC and FEF.	Applicable but lack compelling evidence
	Shin *et al*., 2019 50-min driving simulation	Smart phone system	The concentration of salivary cortisol: low level indicates fatigue	saliva was collected at the end of each test (5-min practice and three 15-min driving tests)	Applicable but requires the control of confounding factors (stress)
	cognitive tasks (a review in Lee *et al*., 2021)	Smart watch /Electrocardiograph	Heart rate variability	increased high-frequency power and decreased low-frequency power	Applicable
	Qiao *et al*., 2016 Driving test	Eye tracker	Increased blink duration & frequency, delay of lid reopening	Standardised	Applicable when stress-related factors are controlled
	Zhu *et al* Ji, 2004 Driving test		Increased ratio of eye closure and average eye closure speed		Applicable for extremely lengthy or taxing tasks

Cognitive/ mental fatigue	Munoz-de-Escalona et al., 2020 aircraft tasks	Eye tracker	Reduced pupil size	baseline correction of pupil-size	Applicable if confounding factors (*e.g.*, task difficulty, emotionality of source texts) are controlled
	Rasyad *et al.*, 2020 1-hour computer-based work	Eye link II	Saccades, eye blink frequency and duration	fatigue occurs from 30-40 min, microsleep from 40-50 min; eye blink variables are more sensitive than saccades	
General fatigue	Zhu & Ji, 2004 Test of Attention	Facial expression detector	lagging facial muscles, expressionless, and frequent yawning	multi-scale and multi-orientation Gabor wavelets are used to represent and detect facial features	Only applicable in extremely lengthy or taxing tasks
	Zhang *et al.*, 2014 2h simulated driving	Human observation	Signs of boredom, anxiety, agitation, restlessness, or grimace; yawn and doze		

Table 1: Physiological Indicators of Fatigue in Previous Literature.

Translation can induce both muscular and cognitive fatigues. For the former, thin, and high-resolution sensors or EMG electrodes can be placed on the skin surfaces where translators exercise continuous forces such as thenar to detect physical fatigue caused by typing. Meanwhile, cameras and EOG can be combined to document changes in translators' facial expressions (e.g., face lagging) and eye movements (increased eye blink frequency and duration, and decreased eyelid muscle activities indicate visual fatigue), which serve as indicators of facial muscular fatigue. As to cognitive fatigue, attention decrement and drowsiness can be monitored by portable EEG cap (fatigue is indexed by an increase in theta and alpha frequency band and a decrease in beta frequency band), fMRI (indicated by changes in network connectivity between different brain regions), or eye trackers (a decrease in pupil size, eye closure speed, or an increase in the percentage of eye closure and saccades). However, it merits notice that when applying aforesaid biomarkers, confounding factors must be considered in the experimental design. For instance, when using pupil size as an indicator of fatigue, environmental (e.g., light, noise), task (e.g., time pressure), textual (e.g., difficulty and emotionality of source texts) and personal (e.g., health condition, medication and coffee consumption) factors should be controlled for a between-period comparison as evidence shows that pupil dilation is sensitive to those elements (Hvelplund & Lehr, 2021). Moreover, to ensure those physiological changes result from fatigue, time on task is essential. The duration of previous experiments ranged from 30 minutes to 8 hours depending on the task workload. And one study conducted in the similar scenario to translation (Rasyad et al., 2020) indicated fatigue due to computer-based work normally occurs after 30-40 minutes. In this sense, translators' fatigue may appear after a similar length of screen-based translation. Researchers interested in this topic should set their studies at a reasonably long time to detect its effect and meanwhile consider individualised factors such as fatigue proneness.

Compared with scales, physiological data collected by those devices have the merits of reflecting the unconscious aspect of fatigue and accurately recording online states. Nevertheless, its flaws are also obvious. Multiple sources of one physiological signal means that it can be hard to make a confident interpretation of changes in interested variables. As fatigue shares some cognitive, physiological and behavioural indicators with demotivation, the following section will discuss how to differentiate fatigue from demotivation based on their conceptual and measurement differences.

3 Definition of (De)motivation and its Measurement

Motivation is a topic of interdisciplinary discussion for which multitudes of theories and models (e.g., self-determination theory, motivational intensity theory) have been established to explicate its operating mechanism. Some treat motivation as a trait which exercises long-term effects on work and learning performance (Deci & Ryan, 1985), while others regarded it as a state that have direct influences over task effort and outcomes (Brehm & Self, 1989). To illustrate how motivation as a trait and a state play their role in cognitive and physical activities, emphasis have been placed on its measurement.

Theoretically speaking, trait motivation composes of intrinsic and extrinsic motivations, which stem from the satisfaction of competence, relatedness, autonomy, and external rewards or regulations (Deci & Ryan, 1985). Contrarily, a failure to meet those requirements entails amotivation/demotivation. Though relatively steady, trait motivation can be domain specific as one's motivation to work is no equivalence of that to learning or entertainments. Moreover, trait motivation is so implicit that its measurement largely relies on established scales. In translation studies, a typical example is interpreter trainers' learning (de)motivation scale (Wu, 2016). In comparison, state motivation is temporary and task-specific, whose intensity is believed to have detectable cognitive, behavioural and physiological outcomes (Blaise et al., 2021; Derbali & Frasson, 2010; Neigel et al., 2019). Defined strictly, state motivation is regulated by the biological structure of Basal Ganglia and its intensity can shift even within one single task (Wasserman & Wasserman, 2020). In practice, state motivation is always interchangeably used with task motivation and operates as a multi-component structure (de Brabander & Martens, 2014). As such, the more prudent measurement is a combination of self-report and biometric data. Regarding self-report data, factors such as self-efficacy, autonomy, task meaning, utility, enjoyment, and difficulty, as well as output satisfaction are theoretically presumed as reflections of task motivation (Kormos & Wilby, 2019). As to biomarkers, motivational intensity theory (Brehm & Self, 1989) proposes task effort as an indicator of task motivation which can be measured by sympathetic system responses in systolic blood pressure and pre-ejection period. Ideally, task motivation would increase as tasks get more complicated if task accomplishment is possible and justified. And enhanced motivation is indicated by a higher level of systolic blood pressure and shorter pre-ejection period. By contrast, when task difficulty exceeds one's competence, a sense of demotivation would entail a sharp decline in task effort, thus lowering systolic blood pressure and lengthening pre-ejection period. Empirical evidence from varied cognitive and physical tasks have lent adequate validity to those assumptions (Guido et al., 2012). Although SBP and PEP are most suitable measures of motivational intensity from a biological angle, alternative indices such as diastolic blood pressure, heart rate, pupil size and skin conductance are also utilised in many experiments in case one indicator may be insensitive to certain stimuli. Of note is that current practice measures task motivation holistically and focuses on differences in selected parameters between pre-task and during-task conditions rather than subperiods in one lengthy task. Specifically, task motivation is calculated as the mean level of biological data over the whole task deducted by baseline data collected at the resting condition.

More recently, EEG has also been applied to record motivational states (Gergelyfi et al., 2015) since changes of band power in the prefrontal cortex proved to be modulated by emotion and motivation (Spielberg et al., 2008). Specifically, approach motivation leads to more activations in the left hemisphere whereas withdrawal motivation activates the right hemisphere more (Gollan et al., 2014, Horan et al., 2014). And more motivating tasks produce greater magnitude EEG alpha and beta band power in the left prefrontal cortex (Sammler et al., 2007). With the growing application of EEG, channels corresponding to attention, emotion, motivation, and fatigue were further identified. Moreover, using residual-to-residual CNN algorithm, beta waves proved to outperform alpha waves in the accurate predication of motivation for game-playing (Chattopadhyayet al., 2021).

Motivation type	Author, date & instruments	Application scenarios	Dimensions & indications	Measurement features & cautions when applied
Trait motivation	Wu 2016 Interpretation learning motivation scale	Motivation for learning interpretation	Motivation and demotivation	Theory-based and data-driven scale. Require administration immediately before or after the investigated period as participants' responses can vary noticeably across time
	Cai & Dong 2017 Interpretation learning motivation scale		Intrinsic motive, instrumental motive, achievement goal, intended effort	
	Wu 2019 Translation learning motivation scale	Motivation for learning translation	Attitudes to learning environment, teachers and translation, interest in translation, willingness to translate	Modified motivation scale with no distinction between intrinsic and extrinsic motivations
	Amabile *et al.*1994 Work preference inventory	Professionals' work motivation or students' learning motivation	Intrinsic (challenge & enjoyment) and extrinsic (outward & compensation) motivations	Widely applied; requiremodifications to make the scale more relevant to translation work, scale validation in different cultures has generated different subdimensions (Ocal *et al.*, 2019)
State motivation	Carver & White 1994 BIS/BAS scale	Simple cognitive tasks	Approach (reward responsiveness, drive, and fun seeking) & Avoidance motivations: lower score indicates low motivation	Have been validated and applied in different cultures; validation of this scale in different contexts has led to different subdimensions (Maack & Ebesutani, 2018)
	Task-specific motivation scale *e.g.*, Martin (2012)'s English Writing Motivation and Engagement Scale	(L2) writing task	Self-belief, anxiety, task value, learning focus, persistence, uncertain control, task management, disengagement, planning, failure avoidance and self-sabotage	Situational but subjective, for whose implementation individual differences should be considered
	Heart rate-related variables (*e.g.*, pre-ejection period)	Simple cognitive and physical tasks	difference in indicators between the resting and the operating states: a reduced difference indicates declined motivation	Spontaneous and simultaneous. Hard to interpret if confounding factors (*e.g.*, emotional source texts) were not strictly controlled; may not be so sensitive in certain conditions and better used combinedly
	Blood pressure	Cognitive tasks		
	Skin conductance	Cognitive tasks		
	EEG	Cognitive tasks		Sophisticated operation and calculation

Table 2: Applied/applicable motivation measurements for translation activities

As shown in Table2, in translation studies, previous investigators have adopted theories and models in the learning domain to develop their scales and confined their targets on language learners. However, as professional translators' motivation has been found to shape their performance (Lehr, 2014), trait and state motivation measurements dedicated to translation are in urgent demand if further exploration of the underlying mechanism were conducted. In this sense, pre-existing generic scales (e.g., work preference inventory, BAS/BIS scale), though not directly applicable, lay the foundation for translation scholars to build their measurement toolkits. Take WPI as an example, the general expression that "I love tackling problems completely new to me" can be situationalised by adding "translation" before "problems". Moreover, as exploratory factor analysis in previous studies on employers' motivation has generated structures different from the original ones, it is essential to validate the modified scales with adequate sample size before their implementation. Regarding state motivation, psychological metrics (e.g., blood pressure, heart rate variables, skin conductance) widely applied in other cognitive tasks are worthy of consideration if confounding factors (e.g., emotional valence of source texts) were meticulously controlled. Another two cautions are: 1). when the attentional and emotional aspects of translation are concurrently examined, eye-movement indicators such as pupil size may not be a rigorous biomarker; 2). in practice, some biomarkers may not be so sensitive to motivational alteration, for which a combined use of indexes are recommended.

4 How to Differentiate Fatigue and Demotivation in Translation

In theory, demotivation and fatigue is easily distinguishable. The former is a physical and mental state out of personal control, while the latter is more related to one's willingness and are thus largely self-determined. However, concerning their measurements, the boundary becomes less clear-cut. Not only fatigue can be a source of demotivation, but also demotivation and fatigue share some cognitive (less focused) and behavioural (underperformance) signals. The theoretical premise that the amount of deliberate effort, efficiency of attention allocation and information processing can index one's motivation fails to discriminate demotivation from fatigue which could lead to same outcomes, albeit at an unconscious level. In this regard, the employment of traditional scales, though at the risk of inaccuracy and latency, seems more helpful in differentiating physical states from emotional states than biomarkers of attention and effort.

However, a perusal of theoretical and biological underpinnings for their measurements sheds more lights. First, fatigue is an exhausting state due to protracted work, which means long time-on-task is a requisite to its occurrence. Differently, lack of motivation can happen at any stage of task performance, either because of one's unwilling to take the task (in the very beginning), a growing understanding of task difficulty (in the middle of task) or gradually getting bored. Second, as one subdimension of fatigue, muscle fatigue has physical features undetectable in the case of demotivation. Biologically speaking, human beings are unlikely to control their muscles in a conscious way, especially in cognitive tasks where skeletal muscle does not play a noted role. In this sense, biometers for measuring muscle fatigue such as EMG and EOG are effective in distinguishing fatigue from demotivation. Third, as far as the mental aspect of both states is concerned, bio-signals of drowsiness (e.g., increased activities in Alpha band power) are peculiar to fatigue as motivation is more self-controlled and operates consciously in most of time. Meanwhile, neuroscience scholars have mapped out some brain regions correspond to motivation and fatigue respectively (Chattopadhyay et al., 2021), which paves the way for applying EEG to tell fatigue from demotivation that may occur at the similar stage. Finally, physiological indices of parasympathetic and sympathetic activities are also useful. Based on motivational intensity theory, demotivation is associated with decreased arousal in sympathetic activities (indicated by lower SBP and longer PEP), which has gained ample empirical supports. Contrarily, fatigue was discovered to be linked to increased sympathetic arousal (Tran et al., 2009) and decreased parasympathetic nervous activities (Lee et al., 2021). Hence, the opposite reflections of those two states in the autonomic nervous system speaks to the applicability of heart rate and blood pressure related parameters for their distinction. Actually, Gergelyfi et al. (2015) have employed a series of neural, autonomic, psychometric, and behavioural signatures to dissociate effects on working memory performance of mental fatigue (measured by ECG, eye blink, and Multidimensional Fatigue Inventory) from that of motivation (measured by EEG, pupil diameter, skin conductance response, and self-rated task interest, efficacy, effort, and value). And their results showed participants' subjective feeling of fatigue is positively related to their eye blink rate and heart rate variability. While reward-induced EEG, pupillometric and skin conductance signal changes (indexes of motivation) did not correlate with subjective and objective indices of mental fatigue. Tentative as their findings are, this research nevertheless indicates the differentiable manifestations of amotivation and fatigue.

5 Conclusion

In summary, although fatigue is a confounding factor that previous translation experiments all try to control, no objective or subjective approaches have been adopted to detect its occurrence. To bridge this gap, this article, based on the fatigue literature, proposed some methods for monitoring and measuring translators' fatigue, which cover self-report scales and various physiological biomarkers. To avoid the impacts of emotional states that share similar cognitive and behavioural consequences with fatigue on its accurate measurement, demotivation was taken as an example to illustrate how to distinguish affective and physical states in translation activities. In doing so, this paper not only illuminates on the measurement of two essential influencers of translation performance, but also cautions on the meticulous employment of biomarkers in translation studies. For future experimenters with an eye on translation (de)motivation and fatigue, it is advised to incorporate objective and subjective measures for the sake of data triangulation. Specifically, PEP and S/DBP, heart rate and skin conductance can be useful indicators of (de)motivation. While muscular activities (in face or body) recorded by EMG, EOG or cameras can help detect translation fatigue. Meanwhile, a combination of biomarkers serves as a safeguard to potential "insensitivity" issue. On the other hand, when scales or self-reports are employed, their relevance to translation tasks, translation (if not phrased in participants' mother tongue) and validation (for both newly developed and established scales) are things to consider.

References

Ackerman, P. L. (2011). 100 Years Without Resting. In *Cognitive Fatigue Multidisciplinary Perspectives on Current Research and Future Applications,* pages 11–44. American Psychological Association.

Ackerman, P. L., & Kanfer, R. (2009). Test length and cognitive fatigue: An empirical examination of effects on performance and test-taker reactions. *Journal of Experimental Psychology*. Applied, 15(2):163–181.

Åhsberg, E. (2000). Dimensions of fatigue in different working populations. *Scandinavian Journal of Psychology*, 41(3), 231–241.

Ani, M. F., Kamat, S., & Fukumi, M. (2020). Development of Decision Support System via ErgonomicsApproach for Driving Fatigue Detection. *Journal of Social Science and Technical Education*,1:60–72.

Antons, J.-N., Schleicher, R., Arndt, S., Moeller, S., & Curio, G. (2012). Too Tired for Calling? A Physiological Measure of Fatigue Caused by Bandwidth Limitations. *2012 Fourth International Workshop on Quality of Multimedia Experience,* 63–67.

Amabile, T. M., Hill, K. G., Hennessey, B. A., & Tighe, E. M. (1994). The Work Preference Inventory:Assessing intrinsic and extrinsic motivational orientations. *Journal of Personality and Social Psychology*, 66(5):950-967.

Balkin, T. J., & Wesensten, N. J. (2011). Differentiation of Sleepiness and Mental Fatigue Effects. In*Cognitive Fatigue: Multidisciplinary Perspectives on Current Research and Future Applications*, pages 47–66. American Psychological Association.

Blaise, M., Marksteiner, T., Krispenz, A., & Bertrams, A. (2021). Measuring Motivation for CognitiveEffort as State. *Frontiers in Psychology*.12: 785094.

Brehm, J. W., & Self, E. A. (1989). The intensity of motivation. *Annual Review of Psychology*, 40:109-131.

Carver, C. S., & White, T. L. (1994). Behavioral inhibition, behavioral activation, and affective responses to impending reward and punishment: The BIS/BAS Scales. *Journal of Personality and Social Psychology,* 67(2): 319-333.

de Brabander, C. J., & Martens, R. L. (2014). Towards a unified theory of task-specific motivation. *Educational Research Review,* 11: 27-44.

Deci, E. L., & Ryan, R. M. (1985). *Intrinsic Motivation and Self-Determination in Human Behavior.* Springer.

Deci, E. L., & Ryan, R. M. (2013). *Intrinsic Motivation and Self-Determination in Human Behavior.* Springer Science & Business Media.

Derbali, L., & Frasson, C. (2010). Prediction of Players Motivational States Using Electrophysiological Measures during Serious Game Play. *2010*

10th IEEE International Conference on Advanced Learning Technologies, 498-502.

Fan, D. (2012). *The Development of Expertise in Interpreting through Self-Regulated Learning for Trainee Interpreters* [PhD Thesis]. University of Newcastle.

Ghasem, M. (2019). Developing and validating involvement in translation scale and its relationship with translation ability. *Forum,* 17(2):225-248.

Guido, H. E., Gendolla, R. A. W., & Michael, R. (2012). Effort Intensity: Some Insights From the Cardiovascular System. In *The Oxford Handbook of Human Motivation*, page 420-440. Oxford University Press, Inc.

Hockey, G. R. (1997). Compensatory control in the regulation of human performance under stress and high workload; a cognitive-energetical framework. *Biological Psychology*, 45(1–3):73-93.

Hockey, G. R. J. (2011). A Motivational Control Theory of Cognitive Fatigue. In *Cognitive Fatigue: Multidisciplinary Perspectives on Current Research and Future Applications*, pages 168-188. American Psychological Association.

Jing, D., Liu, D., Zhang, S., & Guo, Z. (2020). Fatigue driving detection method based on EEG analysis in low-voltage and hypoxia plateau environment. *International Journal of Transportation Science,* 9(4):366-376.

Kanfer, R. (2011). Determinants and Consequences of Subjective Cognitive Fatigue. In *Cognitive Fatigue: Multidisciplinary Perspectives on Current Research and Future Applications*, pages 189-208. American Psychological Association.

Kitanovska-Kimovska, S., & Cvetkoski, V. (2022). The Effect of Emotions on Translation Performance. *Research in Language*, 19:169-186.

Kormos, J. & Wilby, J. (2019). Task Motivation. In *The Palgrave handbook of motivation for language learning*, pages 267-286. Palgrave Macmillan.

Lee, K. F. A., Gan, W.-S., & Christopoulos, G. (2021). Biomarker-Informed Machine Learning Model of Cognitive Fatigue from a Heart Rate Response Perspective. *Sensors*, 21(11):3843.

Lehr, C. (2014). *The influence of emotion on language performance: Study of a neglected determinant of decision-making in professional translators* [PhD Thesis]. Univ. Genève,.

Lehr, C., & Hvelplund, K. T. (2020). Emotional experts: Influences of emotion on the allocation of cognitive resources during translation. *Multilingual Mediated Communication and Cognition*, 44-68.

Maack, D. J., & Ebesutani, C. (2018). A re-examination of the BIS/BAS scales: Evidence for BIS and BAS as unidimensional scales. *International Journal of Methods in Psychiatric Research*, 27(2):e1612.

Martin, A. (2012). Motivation and engagement: Conceptual, operational, and empirical clarity. In *Handbook of research on student engagement*, pages 303-311. Springer.

Muñoz-de-Escalona, E., Cañas, J. J., & Noriega, P. (2020). Inconsistencies between mental fatigue measures under compensatory control theories. *Psicológica Journal*, 41(2):103-126.

Neigel, A. R., Claypoole, V. L., & Szalma, J. L. (2019). Effects of state motivation in overload and underload vigilance task scenarios. *Acta Psychologica,* 197:106-114.

Ocal, F., Akdol, B., & Arikboga, F. S. (2019). The Work Preference Inventory: Motivation Factors of Banking Sector Employees. *Siyasal-Journal of Political Sciences*, 28(2):257-280.

Peng, Y., Li, C., Chen, Q., Zhu, Y., & Sun, L. (2022). Functional Connectivity Analysis and Detection of Mental Fatigue Induced by Different Tasks Using Functional Near-Infrared Spectroscopy. *Frontiers in Neuroscience*, 15:771056.

Punsawad, Y., Aempedchr, S., Wongsawat, Y., & Parnichkun, M. (2015). Weighted-Frequency Index for EEG-based Mental Fatigue Alarm System. *International Journal of Applied Biomedical Engineering*, 4(1):36-41.

Qiao, Y., Zeng, K., Xu, L., & Yin, X. (2016). A smartphone-based driver fatigue detection using fusion of multiple real-time facial features. *2016 13th IEEE Annual Consumer Communications & Networking Conference*, 230-235.

Rahayu, S., Ani, M. F., & Fa'iz, M. (2016). A comparison study for the road condition with hand grip force and muscle fatigue. Malaysian Journal of Public Health Medicine, 1:7-13.

Rasyad, M., Muslim, E., & Pradana, A. A. (2020). Measurement of Fatigue Eye on Computer Users with Method of Eye Tracking. In *Recent Progress on: Mechanical, Infrastructure and Industrial Engineering* (Vol. 2227, p. 040026). Amer Inst Physics.

Richter, M., & Slade, K. (2017). Interpretation of physiological indicators of motivation: Caveats and recommendations. *International Journal of Psychophysiology*, 119:4-10.

Rojo, A., & Caro, M. R. (2016). Can emotion stir translation skill? Defining the impact of positive and negative emotions on translation performance. In *Re-embedding Translation Process Research*, pages 107-130. John Benjamins.

Rojo, A. M., & Korpal, P. (2020). Through your skin to your heart and brain: A critical evaluation of physiological methods in Cognitive Translation and Interpreting Studies. *Linguistica Antverpiensia, New Series – Themes in Translation Studies*, 19:191-217.

Sammler, D., Grigutsch, M., Fritz, T., & Koelsch, S. (2007). Music and emotion: Electrophysiological correlates of the processing of pleasant and unpleasant music. *Psychophysiology*, 44(2):293-304.

Shin, J., Kim, S., Yoon, T., Joo, C., & Jung, H.-I. (2019). Smart Fatigue Phone: Real-time estimation of driver fatigue using smartphone-based cortisol detection. *Biosensors and Bioelectronics*,136:106-111.

Spielberg, J. M., Stewart, J. L., Levin, R. L., Miller, G. A., & Heller, W. (2008). Prefrontal Cortex, Emotion, and Approach/Withdrawal Motivation. *Social and Personality Psychology Compass*, 2(1):135-153.

Tran, Y., Wijesuriya, N., Tarvainen, M., Karjalainen, P., & Craig, A. (2009). The Relationship Between Spectral Changes in Heart Rate Variability and Fatigue. *Journal of Psychology*, 23:143-151.

Trejo, L. J., Kochavi, R., Kubitz, K., Montgomery, L. D., Rosipal, R., & Matthews, B. (2005). Measures and models for predicting cognitive fatigue. In *Biomonitoring for Physiological and Cognitive Performance During Military Operations*, pages 105-115. Spie-Int Soc Optical Engineering.

Wasserman, T., & Wasserman, L. (2020). Motivation: State, Trait, or Both. In *Motivation, Effort, and the Neural Network Model*, pages 93-101. Springer International Publishing.

Weng, Y., & Zheng, B. (2020). A multi-methodological approach to studying time-pressure in written translation: Manipulation and measurement. *Linguistica Antverpiensia New Series-Themes in Translation Studies*, 19:218-236.

Wu, G. (2019). A study on the motivation and its effects in translation learning among English majors. *Foreign Language Education*, 40(2):66-70.

Wu, Z. (2016). Towards understanding interpreter trainees' (de)motivation: An exploratory study. *Translation and Interpreting: The International Journal of Translation and Interpreting Research,* 8:13-25.

Zhang, C., Wang, H., & Fu, R. (2014). Automated Detection of Driver Fatigue Based on Entropy and Complexity Measures. Intelligent Transportation Systems. *IEEE Transactions,*15:168-177.

Zhu, Z., & Ji, Q. (2004). Real time and non-intrusive driver fatigue monitoring. *Proceedings. The 7th International IEEE Conference on Intelligent Transportation Systems*, 657-662.

Zhang, J., Xu, J. W., & Wang, W. C. (2004). Construct research on work motivation of Chinese employees. In *Management Sciences and Global Strategies in the 21st Century*, pages 1876-1881. Macao Univ Science Technology.

Investigating the Impact of Different Pivot Languages on Translation Quality

Longhui Zou lzou4@kent.edu
Ali Saeedi asaeedi@kent.edu
Michael Carl mcarl6@kent.edu
Modern and Classical Language Studies, Kent State University, Kent, USA

Abstract

Translating via an intermediate pivot language is a common practice, but the impact of the pivot language on the quality of the final translation has not often been investigated. In order to compare the effect of different pivots, we back-translate 41 English source segments via various intermediate channels (Arabic, Chinese and monolingual paraphrasing) into English. We compare the 912 English back-translations of the 41 original English segments using manual evaluation, as well as COMET and various incarnations of BLEU. We compare human from-scratch back-translations with MT back-translations and monolingual paraphrasing. A variation of BLEU (Cum-2) seems to better correlate with our manual evaluation than COMET and the conventional BLEU Cum-4, but a fine-grained qualitative analysis reveals that differences between different pivot languages (Arabic and Chinese) are not captured by the automatized TQA measures.

1 Introduction

Translation via a pivot language has been a common practice for a long time. For instance, the preservation of ancient Greek ideas is a major contribution of Islamic civilization via Arabic as a pivot language. Much of Aristotle's original work in Old Greek is preserved to us through Muslim scholars who translated the ancient-Greek scripts into Arabic which was then later translated into Latin, and from there into various other languages. Still today, pivot translation is an important technique mainly due to a lack of available direct translators. The availability of translators who know two (or more) languages becomes increasingly limited as the number of speakers in those languages decreases. It is, therefore, in particular, translation across smaller languages which requires translation via another, usually a more common language. Thus, from the more than 4000 languages in the world that have developed a writing system [1], translators will be available for only a very tiny fraction of the 16 million or so possible language combinations. However, translations into (or out of) the 'big' languages — such as English, French, Spanish, Russian, or Arabic — might be more easily available. Similarly, there are 552 language pairs for the 24 official European languages but it might not always be possible to find translators for all of these combinations. As a work-around, often English, French, or Spanish are used as an intermediate language in the EU.

While pivot translation is commonly used for written and spoken language (e.g., Interpretation), not much work exists that assesses the impact of the intermediate language on the translation quality. Pieta (2019) indicates that translation studies researchers' interest in pivot

[1] https://www.ethnologue.com/

translation has grown since the mid-2010s. The first research that focuses on pivot translation, however, can be traced back to 1963 which was in regard to literary works (Zaborov, 1963). Zaborov's work reflects the Soviets authorial control over book translation by requiring to translate any foreign book into Russian before it can be translated into other languages (Pieta, 2019). Translation studies' trend of literature-oriented research focusing on pivot translation carried on through the seventies, eighties and nineties of the twentieth century (Radó, 1975; Toury, 1988; aus zweiter Hand, 1984; DURISIN, 1991; Kurtz and Pöhlker, 1999). Starting from 1999 onward, pivot translation research expanded to include two other areas in which translation via an intermediate language is considered a common practice, namely interpreting and audiovisual translation (Gambier, 2003; Zilberdik, 2004; Shlesinger, 2010). More recently, pivot translation is getting more popular in more areas of research. Liu et al. (2018) for instance, review the applicability of pivot MT systems and recommend incorporating "quality estimation and/or automatic/human post-editing to the intermediate translation of the pivot language" (p. 10). Most recently, O'Hagan (2022) investigates the challenges, and implications of the use of English pivot translation in game localization.

The choice of the pivot language is often based on the available human (and/or electronic) resources, but the quality of the final translation depends crucially on the quality of the pivot language. If there is a mistake or ambiguity in the pivot translation, the source meaning might be erroneously or incompletely reproduced in the target. The pivot language might be lacking (linguistic) constructions and possibilities that the source language has and, therefore, be incorrectly recovered from the pivot language. The pivot language might also favor interpretations that lead to incorrect conclusions in the target. As compared to direct translation, pivot translation proceeds in two step (1: source-to-pivot and 2:pivot-to-target), each of which filters or amplifies the linguistic signal in specific ways.

In this study, we use back-translation as a method to assess the impact of different pivot languages in translation. We choose the source and the target to be the same language (English), and we select two quite different pivot languages, Chinese and Arabic. Back-translation into English via two different intermediate languages allows us to clearly assess the impact of the pivot language, since any divergence between the source and the target can be attributed to the intermediate language. We triangulate using monolingual paraphrasing as a tool with which back-translations are compared.

Section 2 provides a detailed description of the different datasets and their collection processes. In Section 3, we explain the different translation quality assessment methods we used. We describe our manual evaluation design and use its result as a reference for the results of the two automatic evaluation metrics we incorporate (BLEU and COMET). Then, we draw quantitative and qualitative comparisons among the three assessment metrics' results. In Section 4, we present a statistically backed discussion of the influence of pivot languages on human translation quality in our datasets. We follow this discussion with an in-depth qualitative observations from our datasets in the light of normalization, priming, and shining-through. Section 5 gives a summary and conclusions and states future endeavors.

2 Experimental Design

This study compares English back-translations via Arabic and Chinese pivot languages and monolingual English paraphrasing on the segment level. We generated data for from-scratch back-translation (HT) via Arabic (AR), Chinese (ZH), via monolingual English paraphrasing (PH), as well as machine back-translation (MT).

A total number of 41 English source segments were first machine translated and post-edited by professional translators into Arabic and Chinese. These Arabic and Chinese translations served as pivot translation. Subsequently, the Arabic pivot translations were then back-translated into English by 8 translators (AR) - with Arabic as their first language (L1) and English as their second language (L2). The Chinese pivot translations were back-translated into English by 4 translators (ZH) - with Chinese as their L1 and English as their L2. For these human from-scratch back-translations, we collected behavioral data, eye-tracking and key logging.

As described in (Saeedi, 2021), we also used two neural machine translation (NMT) systems (i.e., Bing and Google Translate) to generate English NMT back-translations (MT) via the Arabic and Chinese pivot translations. In addition, 8 computer sciences graduate students with English as their L2 produced monolingual paraphrases of the original English segments (EN). A total of 912 translated segments were generated, consisting of: AR 328 segments, ZH 164 segments, MT also 164 segments, from which 82 segments for Arabic (MT-AR) and 82 segments for Chinese (MT-ZH), and EN 256 segments. Figure 1 illustrates this data collection process. It shows how we set up the Translation Quality Assessment (TQA) for three different translation tasks (HT, MT, PH). [2]

The data was processed in the CRITT Translation Process Research Database (Carl et al., 2016, CRITT TPR-DB), which includes manual word-alignment of the 912 segments. The quality of all translated segments were manually evaluated, as well as automatic assessment (i.e., BLEU and COMET). These assessment results were utilized as references for the translation quality.

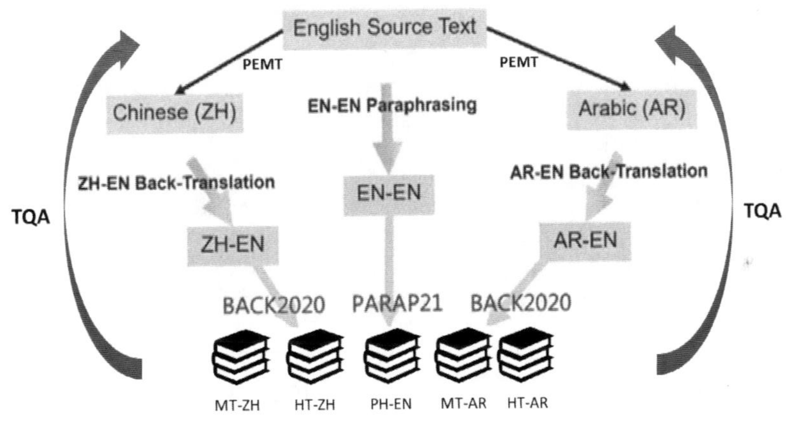

Figure 1: Collection Process of BACK2020 and PARAP21 Datasets

3 Translation Quality Assessment

3.1 Manual evaluation

Manual evaluation is often used as a gold-standard reference to which the performance of automatic metrics are gauged (Papineni et al., 2002; Rei et al., 2020). Several studies proposed criteria for manual evaluation, such as accuracy and fluency (White and O'Connell, 1994; Koehn

[2]MultiLing was used as English source texts (https://sites.google.com/site/centretranslationinnovation/tpr-db/public-studies). Data of paraphrases are gathered in the study PARAP21 while the back-translations are available as BACK2020 in the CRITT TPR-DB.

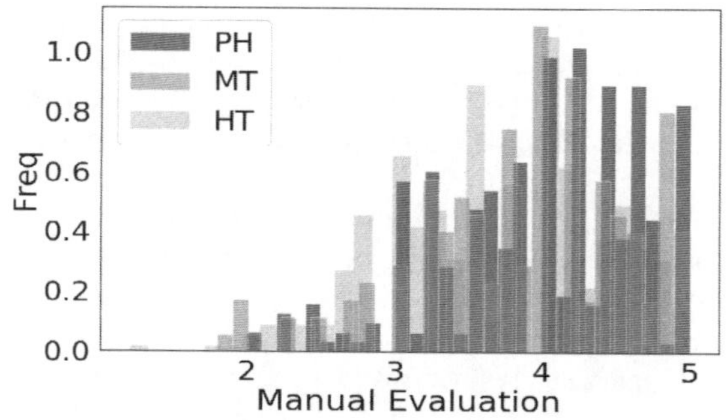

Figure 2: Distribution of Manual Evaluation Scores for Different Translation Tasks: Paraphrasing (PH), Machine Translation (MT), human from-scratch back-translation (HT)

and Monz, 2006; Graham et al., 2015; Barrault et al., 2019; Popović, 2020; Zou et al., 2021). In our study, we select adequacy (i.e., accuracy and fidelity) criteria in view of the fact that accuracy errors are the most severe and often most difficult to detect (White and O'Connell, 1994; Callison-Burch, 2007; Dorr et al., 2010).

Twenty fluent English speakers were recruited as raters, and the evaluation was carried out by rating the (English) back-translations and paraphrasing segments against the (English) source segments according to a likert scale (see Appendix A). Each of the 41 source segments was shown to the raters with 5 candidate translations, and each of the translation segments was rated by 5 raters in different permutations. The inter-rater agreement among all raters was then calculated using the weighted Fleiss's Kappa metric, which showed a good overall agreement of 0.67 (McHugh, 2012).

As a gold standard for segment quality, we used the average manual evaluation score. The distribution of the average manual evaluation per segment for the three translation tasks (i.e., PH, MT, HT) is shown in Figure 2. Evaluators gave overall best scores for PH (μ=3.97, SD=0.68), followed by MT (μ=3.90, SD=0.70), and somewhat less scores to HT (μ=3.64, SD=0.70) in our experiment.

3.2 BLEU

The Bilingual Evaluation Understudy (BLEU) is perhaps the most commonly used automatic metric in TQA research (Doddington, 2002; Dorr et al., 2011; Moorkens et al., 2018). BLEU produces a score between 0 and 1, based on a precision measure that compares n-grams in candidate translations to matching n-grams in reference translations. Specifying the weighting of different n-grams in the calculation of the BLEU score allows for the formation of different types of BLEU scores including individual and cumulative scores. The individual n-gram BLEU scores evaluate the matching grams between the candidate translations and the reference text independently. The cumulative n-gram BLEU scores (referred to as Cum-n) calculate "individual n-gram scores at all orders from 1 to n" and weigh them "by calculating the weighted geometric mean" (Brownlee, 2017). The cumulative 4-gram BLEU score (Cum-4) is the default calculated score for sentence-level or whole-text-level scores (Hailu et al., 2020).

It seems that TQA research seldom delves into different weights of BLEU scores and how they affect the assessment results. We used the `sentence_bleu` function in python to investigate how different configurations of BLEU scores correlate with our manual gold standard evaluation. We calculated the correlation between the BLEU scores and the average manual evaluation for each segment. As we can see from Table 1, 1-gram and Cum-2 scores

	1-gram	2-gram	3-gram	4-gram	Cum-2	Cum-3	Cum-4	COMET	Manual
1-gram	1.0	0.9	0.82	0.73	0.94	0.88	0.81	0.53	0.43
2-gram	0.9	1.0	0.96	0.88	0.98	0.98	0.93	0.46	0.4
3-gram	0.82	0.96	1.0	0.96	0.91	0.97	0.97	0.4	0.37
4-gram	0.73	0.88	0.96	1.0	0.82	0.88	0.95	0.33	0.34
Cum-2	0.94	0.98	0.91	0.82	1.0	0.96	0.89	0.49	0.41
Cum-3	0.88	0.98	0.97	0.88	0.96	1.0	0.94	0.45	0.38
Cum-4	0.81	0.93	0.97	0.95	0.89	0.94	1.0	0.38	0.36
COMET	0.53	0.46	0.4	0.33	0.49	0.45	0.38	1.0	0.37
Manual	0.43	0.4	0.37	0.34	0.41	0.38	0.36	0.37	1.0

All correlations are significant with $p < 0.01$

Table 1: Pearson Correlation Between Different Weights of BLEU Scores, COMET, and Manual Evaluation

correlate best with our manual evaluation results. The correlation coefficients show a moderate relationship between 1-gram (r=0.43), Cum-2 (r=0.41) scores, and manual evaluation (Schober et al., 2018). Given these results, we take it that Cum-2 may be a better assessment method than the commonly used Cum-4. Even though 1-gram provides even better correlation with the human gold-standard assessment, we rule out uni-grams as a viable automatic assessment method as it does not take into consideration any collocational information in the evaluation. Thus we use Cum-2 scores as our selected BLEU weight for segment-level quality assessment. [3]

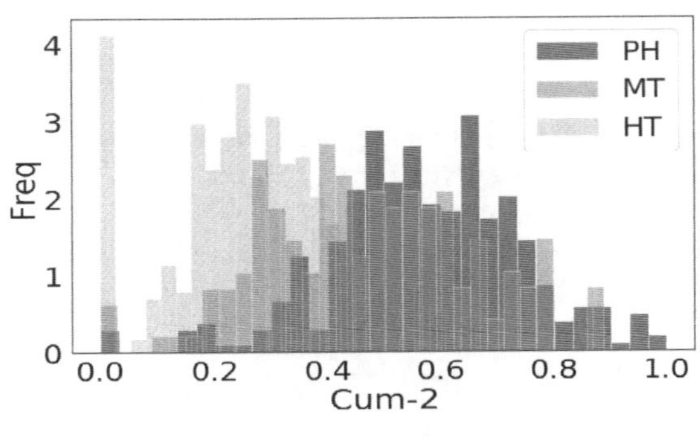

Figure 3: Distribution of BLEU Scores for PH, MT, and HT

We also compare the distributions for Cum-2 scores for the 912 translation segments across the three tasks (HT, MT, PH). As can be gathered from Figure 3, Cum-2 apparently does discriminate between the three translation tasks. Paraphrasing (PH) has overall highest Cum-2 scores (μ=0.57, SD=0.17), followed by MT (μ=0.47, SD=0.19), while human from-scratch back-translation (HT) receives the lowest scores (μ=0.27, SD=0.15). Note that this Cum-2 ranking coincides with the manual evaluation, as in Figure 2, although the discrimination is not as strong in our gold standard.

[3]While larger n-gram may have been useful for earlier MT output to assess fluency issues, shorter n-grams models may better capture translation accuracy. However, with increased quality of recent (N)MT, the main translation problems are due to lack of accuracy.

3.3 COMET

COMET is a neural framework for machine translation evaluation. It can be used to "help evaluate and predict the quality of machine-generated translations for many different languages" (Lavie, 2020). It makes use of word embeddings, which are real-valued vector spaces that encode the meaning (i.e. usage) of the word in context, assuming that words closer in the vector space are expected to be similar in meaning (Teller, 2000). Within COMET, word embeddings "are then passed through a pooling layer to create a sentence embedding for each segment. Finally, the resulting sentence embeddings are combined and concatenated into one single vector that is passed to a feed-forward regressor" (Rei et al., 2020, p. 3). COMET is supposed to better deal with synonymous words, as they are used in similar contexts and thus assigned similar weights. COMET is still a relatively new and understudied automatic assessment metric in TQA research as compared to BLEU.

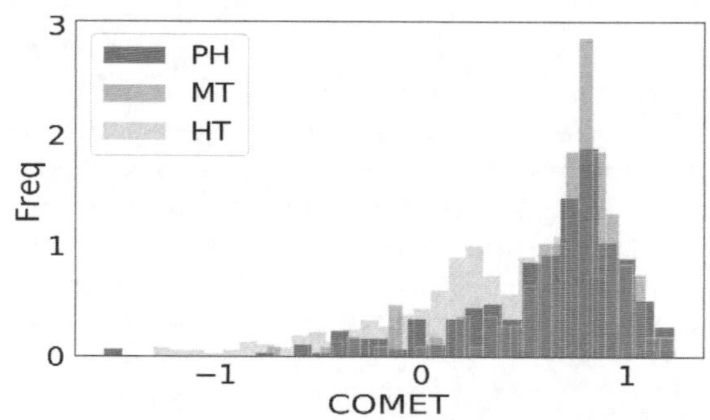

Figure 4: Distribution of COMET Scores for PH, MT, and HT

As illustrated in Table 1, both COMET and manual evaluation correlate best with Cum-2. However, Cum-2 better correlates with our manual evaluation than COMET and the conventional Cum-4. Similar to manual evaluation (section 2) and the BLEU score (section 3), we compare the distribution of COMET scores per segment for the three translation tasks (i.e., PH, MT, HT), as shown in Figure 4. In contrast to the gold standard and Cum-2, COMET gives (on average) highest scores for MT (μ=0.68, SD=0.33) followed by HT (μ=0.59, SD=0.43), then PH (μ=0.30, SD=0.48).

3.4 Comparing Evaluation Metrics

In this section we look at results of the different evaluation methods on a more granular level. Table 2 provides an example that assesses differences between the three evaluation metrics against candidate translations from HT, MT, and PH.

For the HT translation, the Cum-2 score of 0.25 is slightly lower than the Cum-2 average (μ=0.27) for this task, which is likely due to the lack in overlap of uni- and bi-grams between the reference and the candidate translation.

The COMET score (0.68) and the manual evaluation (4.0) for this translation are, in contrast, above their average HT scores of μ=0.30 and μ=3.64 respectively. An explanation for this different assessment may be that COMET and manual evaluation account for semantic similarities rather than the similarity of the words' surface forms. In section 4 we argue that back-translations are less literal than paraphrases or MT (see also Appendix B). Thus, the words *possibly* and *for* in the HT translation can be seen synonymous respectively for *could* and *to* of the reference.

The BLEU Cum-2 scores for other translations (MT and PH) are clearly above the task

Reference	All of them could be considered a burden to hospital staff.			
Task	**Candidate Translation Segment**	**Cum-2**	**COMET**	**Manual**
HT	These victims were possibly considered as the burdens for the hospital staff.	0.25	0.68	4.0
MT	Each of them could be considered a burden on the hospital staff.	0.72	0.74	4.8
PH	He considered all of the a burden to hospital staff.	0.64	0.81	3.8

Table 2: Quality Assessment Scores for Example (1) Among Different Tasks of Translation

average (μ=0.47 and μ=0.57, respectively) which may be due to a larger overlap in word forms. All COMET scores of the translations in Table 2 rank above the task averages. Only the manual evaluation sore (3.8) for the paraphrase is below the task average (μ=3.97). A value of 3.8 falls under the description "some meaning is retained" (see Appendix A). This somewhat lower ranking of the paraphrase can be explained by the typo introduced, *the* instead *them*, and the omission of *could*, both of which does not seem to bother COMET and Cum-2 much.

4 Impact of Different Pivot Languages on Human Translation

In this section we look into differences between paraphrasing (EN) and different human translations via the pivot languages (AR and ZH).

4.1 Distribution of Quality Scores

All three evaluation methods provide relatively higher ratings for paraphrasing (EN) as compared to the Arabic and Chinese back-translations. For manual evaluation, the averages for English paraphrasing (EN, μ=3.97) are significantly higher ($p=9.28e\text{-}10<.01$) than for Chinese (ZH, μ=3.66) and for Arabic (AR, μ=3.63). Moreover, for all three evaluation methods, the distributions of AR and ZH are more similar while EN is set apart. This similarity of distributions can be observed in Figure 5 for all three evaluation methods, manual evaluation, BLEU (Cum-2) and COMET.

Higher scores for paraphrasing may be attributed to the priming effect of the English source language. Stronger priming effects can be expected if the prime is more similar to the target. Carl and Schaeffer (2017) discussed priming effects in post-editing (PEMT) and from-scratch translation. They found that "PEMT produces more literal translations than from-scratch translation" (p. 53), due to the fact that MT output is in almost every aspect closer to the final translation than the ST. A similar effect may be expected for monolingual paraphrasing which resembles PEMT, in some sense, as the prime and the target are in same language in both cases. Monolingual paraphrasing might thus render the target segments more literal as compared to the back-translations. The higher degree of literality — in turn — may explain the higher quality ratings since there may be less variation in surface forms which are closer to the source.

4.2 Translation Variation

In this section we look into the translation variation produced in the different (EN, AR, ZH) channels. As Table 3 shows, back-translations seem to introduce more variation, while English paraphrasing yields more literal renditions. Table 3 plots an English reference sentence and different ways in which the ST word *nomadic* was rendered via paraphrasing and the back-translations. While there is much variation in the back-translations, all 8 monolingual paraphrases make use of different derivations of the same lexeme *nomad*. The literal rendition,

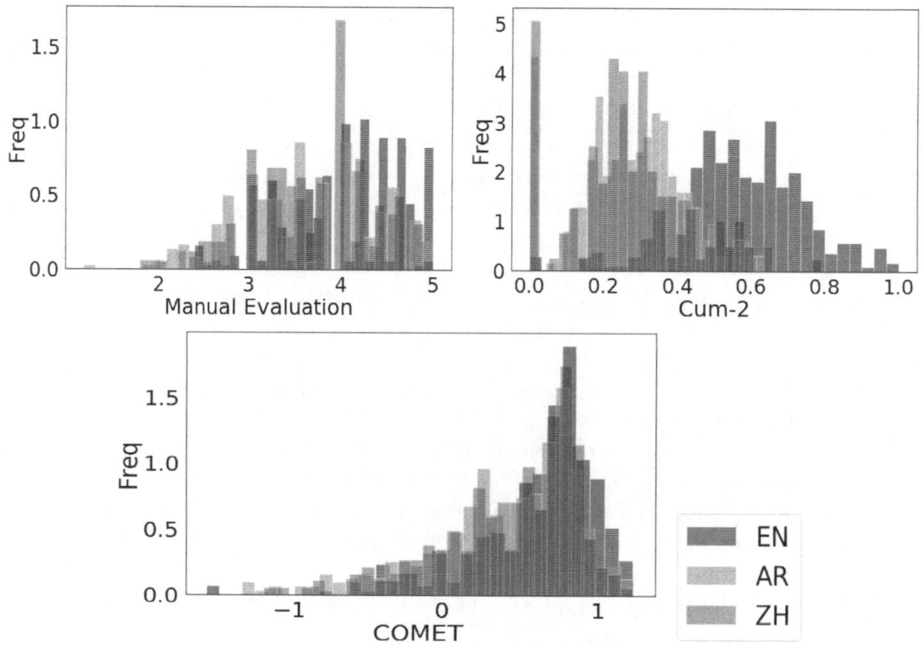

Figure 5: Distribution of manual evaluation scores, BLEU (Cum-2) and COMET for Paraphrasing (EN), back-translation via Arabic (AR) and Chinese (ZH). EN has highest scores and is more clearly separated from the back-translations for all metrics.

nomadic, occurs in 5 out of 8 instances (62.5%). The other 3 instances only change the part of speech, *nomads*, or grammatical number, *nomadics*, albeit incorrectly. This observation corroborates our priming assumption, which suggests that stronger priming effects in monolingual paraphrasing results in more literal translations (see also appendix B).

Carl and Schaeffer (2017) found that there is "more lexical variation in from-scratch translations than in post-editing" (p. 55). In addition, back-translations draw from one extra step of forward translation, which has the potential to introduce more synonymous in the translation. The word *bedouin* is used in 5 out of 8 (62.5%) different back-translations from Arabic with different spellings. This is most likely due to the Arabic pivot translation *min al-mujtama'at al-badawiia al-raHala*, which translates into "of the Bedouin nomadic societies". The word *badawī* in Arabic refers to the nomadic Arab of the desert.

Amponsah-Kaakyire et al. (2021) state that "information about native language and qualifications of the translator is [...] relevant" when analyzing multilingual corpora to study translationese including "language independent characteristics like simplification, normalization, explicitation and avoiding repetitions ... [and] language-pair specific features" like "shining-through of source language patterns in target text" (p. 1). Taking into account that the Arabic pivot translation was produced by a professional translator into his L1, we assume that the word choice "based on [their] subjectivity, is a part of normalization process" (Imjidee and Kwee, 2020, p. 1). The 5 instances of occurrences of *bedouin* in the back-translations suggest thus a shining-through of Arabic pivot translation.

Reference	The majority of hunter-gatherer societies are *nomadic.*		
Pivot	**TT Token(s)**	**Frequency**	**Percentage**
AR	nomadic	3	37.5%
	bedouin nomads	1	12.5%
	bedouin, nomad communities	1	12.5%
	once of the Beduin traveller comunities	1	12.5%
	types of the Beduin traveller communities	1	12.5%
	beduins	1	12.5%
ZH	nomadic	2	50.0%
	moving	1	25.0%
	drift from place to place	1	25.0%
EN	nomadic	5	62.5%
	nomadics	2	25.0%
	nomads	1	12.5%

Table 3: Human Translations for "nomadic" from Pivot Languages and Monolingual Paraphrasing

4.3 Shining through

Teich (2003) stipulates that "what makes translation different from original texts in the same language as the target language is that the source language shines through in translations" (p. 219). Lapshinova-Koltunski (2015) hypothesize that the languages with a higher status tend to 'shine through' more often assuming that in "translations from English, we would probably observe more "shining through [...] as English has the highest world language status (p. 97). From the quantitative analysis in Figure 5, we see that the influence of our pivot languages (AR and ZH) does not seem to have a measurable effect on translation quality, despite that fact that there are qualitatively very different translation variations. We assume this is due to the cultural differences in these two languages.

Reference	[...] Norris *disliked* working with old people.		
Pivot	**TT Token(s)**	**Frequency**	**Percentage**
AR	hated	2	25.0%
	hated to	1	12.5%
	hatred of	1	12.5%
	hates	1	12.5%
	had got to hate	1	12.5%
	did not like	1	12.5%
	disliking	1	12.5%
ZH	doesn't like	2	50.0%
	do not like	1	25.0%
	did not like to	1	25.0%

Table 4: Back-translations for "disliked" via Arabic and Chinese Pivot Languages

In view of this, we further zoom in to the different AR and ZH translations. Table 4 shows (a part of) a reference sentence with 12 AR and ZH back-translations and the different ways in which the token *disliked*, was reproduced. The majority of the Arabic participants — 6 out of 8 (75%) — translated into "hate", only 2 of them (25%) translated into the equivalent meaning *did not like*, or *disliked*. On the contrary, all the Chinese participants translated into some versions of *not like*. We see this as another example of shining through. From the last two examples, we see that different source languages shine through the target text differently since shining-through is a language-pair specific feature.

5 Conclusion

This study investigates the quality of translations via different pivot languages. In order to allow for seamless comparison of the source and the target, it compares human back-translation, neural machine back-translation, and monolingual paraphrasing from English via Arabic and Chinese back into English. Six short English texts (together 41 sentences) were translated into Arabic and Chinese. The two sets of Arabic and Chinese texts were then back-translated into English by 8 Arabic and 4 Chinese translation students respectively. In addition, we also produced back-translations with two NMT systems, Bing and Google Translate, and the English original texts were also paraphrased by 8 computer sciences students. This amounts to 25 English versions: 1 English original, 8 Arabic and 4 Chinese human back-translations, 2 NMT back-translations from Arabic and 2 from Chinese, and 8 (monolingual) paraphraes. However, as some segments were not translated, paraphrased or lost due to software errors, we were left with 912 translated segments (from potentially 24*41 = 984).

We assessed the quality of the 24 reproduced versions (912 translated segments) on a segment level by comparing each of them with the English original, using two automatic measures (BLEU and COMET) as well as manual evaluation. The manual evaluation was based on a Likert scale (see Appendix A) in which 20 fluent English speakers assessed the similarity between the original and the reproduced versions. Each segment was independently rated by at least five evaluators with good agreement (weighted Fleiss's Kappa of 0.67). We took the average score of the manual evaluations as a gold standard. We also experimented with different weights for various BLEU configurations. Our findings indicate that:

- Monolingual paraphrasing has the best scores across our three evaluation methods.

- NMT back-translations achieved similar quality ratings compared to the human back-translations.

- The BLEU Cum-2 measure correlates better with our (averaged) manual gold evaluations than conventional BLEU Cum-4 and COMET.

- Despite qualitative differences, our automatic metrics cannot separate between different pivot languages (AR and ZH).

We explain the higher scores of monolingual paraphrasing (as compared to bilingual paraphrasing) through stronger priming effect, which results in more literal renderings. In contrast, normalization processes effects could be observed in the forward translation when generating the pivot translation, which we explained as cultural differences in the pivot language, while shining-through effects could be observed in the back-translation. Both phenomena may be factors which results in back-translations to show more lexical variation than paraphrasing.

Further studies can be conducted using other automatic metrics and similar methods applied in this study. Further research can also include more pivot languages and NMT systems. Furthermore, the collected behavioral data of eye tracking and key logging of the human from-scratch back-translations can be utilized for purposes of triangulation and also in future related research.

References

Amponsah-Kaakyire, K., Pylypenko, D., España-Bonet, C., and van Genabith, J. (2021). Do not rely on relay translations: Multilingual parallel direct europarl. In *Proceedings for the First Workshop on Modelling Translation: Translatology in the Digital Age*, pages 1–7.

aus zweiter Hand, Ü. (1984). Rezeptionsvorgänge in der europäischen literatur vom 14. bis zum 18. jahrhundert.

Barrault, L., Bojar, O., Costa-Jussa, M. R., Federmann, C., Fishel, M., and Graham, Y. (2019). Findings of the 2019 conference on machine translation (wmt19). In *Proceedings of ACL*. Association for Computational Linguistics (ACL).

Brownlee, J. (2017). A gentle introduction to calculating the bleu score for text in python. *Section on Deep Language Processing. Accessed August*, 20:2019.

Callison-Burch, C. (2007). *Paraphrasing and translation*. PhD thesis, University of Edinburgh Edinburgh.

Carl, M., Bangalore, S., and Schaeffer, M. (2016). New directions in empirical translation process research. *Heidelberg: Springer International Publishing Switzerland. doi*, 10:978–3.

Carl, M. and Schaeffer, M. J. (2017). Why translation is difficult: A corpus-based study of non-literality in post-editing and from-scratch translation. *HERMES-Journal of Language and Communication in Business (56)*, pages 43–57.

Doddington, G. (2002). Automatic evaluation of machine translation quality using n-gram co-occurrence statistics. In *Proceedings of the second international conference on Human Language Technology Research*, pages 138–145.

Dorr, B., Olive, J., McCary, J., and Christianson, C. (2011). Machine translation evaluation and optimization. In *Handbook of natural language processing and machine translation*, pages 745–843. Springer.

Dorr, B. J., Passonneau, R. J., Farwell, D., Green, R., Habash, N., Helmreich, S., Hovy, E., Levin, L., Miller, K. J., Mitamura, T., et al. (2010). Interlingual annotation of parallel text corpora: a new framework for annotation and evaluation. *Natural Language Engineering*, 16(3):197–243.

DURISIN, D. (1991). Artistic translation in the interliterary process. *TTR Studies in the Text and its Transformations*, 4(1):115–127.

Gambier, Y. (2003). Working with relay: An old story and a new challenge. *Speaking in tongues: Language across contexts and users*, 47:66.

Graham, Y., Baldwin, T., and Mathur, N. (2015). Accurate evaluation of segment-level machine translation metrics. In *Proceedings of the 2015 Conference of the North American Chapter of the Association for Computational Linguistics: Human Language Technologies*, pages 1183–1191.

Hailu, T. T., Yu, J., and Fantaye, T. G. (2020). A framework for word embedding based automatic text summarization and evaluation. *Information*, 11(2):78.

Imjidee, N. and Kwee, S. B. (2020). Normalization techniques for translating cultural-specific expressions. *LSP International Journal*, 7(2):1–18.

Koehn, P. and Monz, C. (2006). Manual and automatic evaluation of machine translation between european languages. In *Proceedings on the Workshop on Statistical Machine Translation*, pages 102–121.

Kurtz, J. and Pöhlker, K. (1999). *De L'Un Au Multiple. Traduction Du Chinois Vers Les Langues Européennes/Translation from Chinese Into European Languages.* Les Editions de la MSH.

Lapshinova-Koltunski, E. (2015). Variation in translation: Evidence from corpora. *New directions in corpus-based translation studies*, 1:93.

Lavie, A. (2020). Why we built comet, a new framework and metric for automated machine translation evaluation.

Liu, C.-H., Silva, C. C., Wang, L., and Way, A. (2018). Pivot machine translation using chinese as pivot language. In *China Workshop on Machine Translation*, pages 74–85. Springer.

McHugh, M. L. (2012). Interrater reliability: the kappa statistic. *Biochemia medica*, 22(3):276–282.

Moorkens, J., Castilho, S., Gaspari, F., and Doherty, S. (2018). Translation quality assessment. *Machine translation: Technologies and applications ser. Cham: Springer International Publishing*, 1:299.

O'Hagan, M. (2022). Indirect translation in game localization as a method of global circulation of digital artefacts: A socio-economic perspective. *Target*.

Papineni, K., Roukos, S., Ward, T., and Zhu, W.-J. (2002). Bleu: a method for automatic evaluation of machine translation. In *Proceedings of the 40th annual meeting of the Association for Computational Linguistics*, pages 311–318.

Pieta, H. (2019). Indirect translation: Main trends in practice and research. *Slovo.ru: Baltic accent*, 10:21–36.

Popović, M. (2020). Relations between comprehensibility and adequacy errors in machine translation output. In *Proceedings of the 24th Conference on Computational Natural Language Learning*, pages 256–264.

Radó, G. (1975). Indirect translation. *Babel*, 21(2):51–59.

Rei, R., Stewart, C., Farinha, A. C., and Lavie, A. (2020). Comet: A neural framework for mt evaluation. *arXiv preprint arXiv:2009.09025*.

Saeedi, A. (2021). Comparing backtranslations across different pivot languages and translation modes. In *Proceedings of The international and interdisciplinary conference on Applied Linguistics and Professional Practice (ALAPP)*, page 18.

Schober, P., Boer, C., and Schwarte, L. A. (2018). Correlation coefficients: appropriate use and interpretation. *Anesthesia & Analgesia*, 126(5):1763–1768.

Shlesinger, M. (2010). Relay interpreting. *Handbook of translation studies*, 1:276–278.

Teich, E. (2003). *Cross-linguistic Variation in System and Text: A Methodology for the Investigation of Translations and Comparable Texts*, volume 5. Walter de Gruyter.

Teller, V. (2000). Speech and language processing: an introduction to natural language processing, computational linguistics, and speech recognition.

Toury, G. (1988). Translating english literature via german and vice versa: A symptomatic reversal in the history of modern hebrew literature. *Die literarische Übersetzung: Stand und Perspektiven ihrer Erforschung*, pages 139–157.

White, J. S. and O'Connell, T. A. (1994). Evaluation in the arpa machine translation program: 1993 methodology. In *Human Language Technology: Proceedings of a Workshop held at Plainsboro, New Jersey, March 8-11, 1994*.

Zaborov, P. (1963). 'literatura-posrednik'v istorii russko-zapadnych literaturnych sviazej xviii-xix vv. *InMezhdunarodnye sviazi russkoj literatury. Sbornik statej, edited byM. Alekseev*, pages 64–85.

Zilberdik, N. J. (2004). Relay translation in subtitling. *Perspectives: Studies in translatology*, 12(1):31–55.

Zou, L., Carl, M., Mirzapour, M., Jacquenet, H., and Vieira, L. N. (2021). Ai-based syntactic complexity metrics and sight interpreting performance. In *International Conference on Intelligent Human Computer Interaction*, pages 534–547. Springer.

Appendices

A Description of manual evaluation

For manual evaluation guidelines, we use a Likert scale with the following values:

5	All meaning is retained
4	Most meaning is retained
3	Some meaning is retained
2	Little meaning is retained
1	No meaning is retained

Table 5: Description of Manual Evaluation Metrics

B Segment-wise Target Source Token Ratio

In order to assess a level of literal (i.e., word-for-word translation) vs. free translation for each of the three tasks, we calculate Target/Source Token Ratio (TSR) for each segment, by dividing the number of tokens in the target segment (TokT) by the number of source tokens (TokS). We can see from Figure 6 that HT has the most TSR variation followed by MT and PH. We take higher TSR variation as an indicator for free translation, and low(er) TSR as indicator for more literal translation. According to the TSR measure more literal translations were produced in PH, followed MT, while HT is least literal.

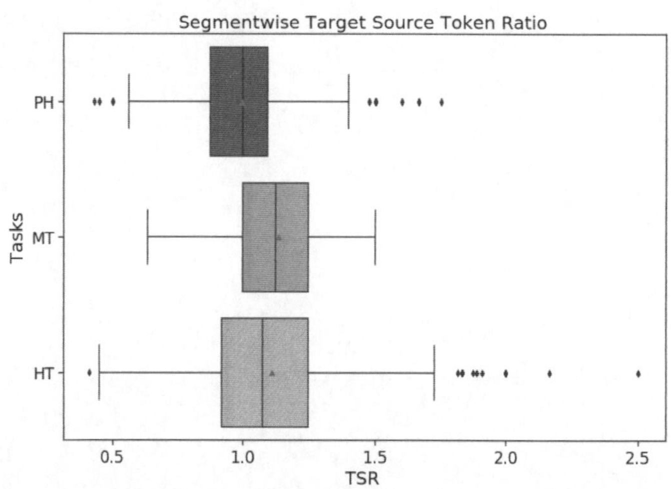

Figure 6: Segment-wise Target Source Token Ratio

Predicting the Number of Errors in Human Translation Using Source Text and Translator Characteristics

Haruka Ogawa ogawaha@earlham.edu
Department of Languages and Cultures, Earlham College, Richmond IN, 47374, USA

Abstract

Translation quality and efficiency are of great importance in the language services industry, which is why production duration and error counts are frequently investigated in Translation Process Research. However, a clear picture has not yet emerged as to how these two variables can be optimized or how they relate to one another. In the present study, data from multiple English-Japanese translation sessions is used to predict the number of errors per segment using source text and translator characteristics. An analysis utilizing zero-inflated generalized linear mixed effects models revealed that two source text characteristics (syntactic complexity and the proportion of long words) and three translator characteristics (years of experience, the time translators spent reading a source text before translating, and the time translators spent revising a translation) significantly influenced the number of errors. Furthermore, a lower proportion of long words per source text sentence and more training led to a significantly higher probability of error-free translation. Based on these results, combined with findings from a previous study on production duration, it is concluded that years of experience and the duration of the final revision phase are important factors that have a positive impact on translation efficiency and quality.

1 Context

In the language services industry, prompt delivery of an accurate translation is greatly appreciated. However, time and quality are often a trade-off, which is a substantial concern for many translators (Mossop, 2014). Although neither human nor machine can create a "perfect" translation instantly, it is important to identify which factors lead to speedy production and high quality. Translation Process Research (TPR) can shed light on such an essential aspect of translation.

In TPR, efficiency has often been investigated with respect to source text (ST) difficulty and the different levels of expertise possessed by translators (i.e., what distinguishes professional translators from non-professionals, such as student translators or language learners). For example, Sharmin et al. (2008) revealed that more difficult texts attracted longer gaze time, and Dragsted (2005) found that difficult STs slowed down production time. Interestingly, in Dragsted's study, professionals tended to fall back on more novice-like behavior when they were engaged in difficult STs, while professionals exhibited exceptional performance when STs were easy. Moreover, research has shown that professional translators produce translations faster than student translators (Dragsted, 2005; Jakobsen and Jensen, 2008). Although the differences in translator behavior based on expertise and ST difficulty are not always statistically significant (see Hvelplund, 2011), the findings in TPR in general support that time efficiency is influenced by the nature of the ST and certain translator characteristics.

While efficiency is relatively easy to define, translation quality is not due to its multi-faceted nature. Product quality can be measured in various ways, for which Garvin (1984) formulated different approaches: the transcendent, product-based, user-based, manufacturing-based, and value-based approaches. In addition to the quality inherent in the product itself, how clients perceive the product is crucial in translation. Indeed, some clients prioritize cost and time over quality. Such being the case, it is hard to reach a consensus as to which aspect of translation quality should be prioritized, although this topic is actively debated in translation industry (Fields et al., 2014).

Quality measurement also poses problems in translation research, though scholars have attempted to take industry perspectives into account. For instance, Colina (2009) introduces a functionalist translation assessment tool that focuses on user points of view. Within the CRITT TPR-DB community,[1] the Multidimensional Quality Metrics (MQM) framework (Lommel, 2018) is often utilized. The CRITT TPR-DB makes it possible to annotate errors using a scheme based on MQM, on a platform called YAWAT (see Germann, 2008; Carl et al., 2016). Although quality measurement based on error typologies such as those made available through MQM has some disadvantages (see O'Brien, 2012; Daems et al., 2013), the error-based assessment of translation can be useful when accuracy is seen as vital (Kivilehto and Salmi, 2017). Such an assessment is also extremely beneficial to TPR in that it offers clarity and consistency to the field.

The complexity of investigating translation quality makes it difficult to fully capture the trade-off or interplay between production time and quality, especially in human translation (HT). However, some interesting findings have been reported. For example, Daems et al. (2016) examined the use of external resources during HT and post-editing (PE) and found that the overall production time of HT was significantly higher than PE due to the increased time spent on external resources in HT. They also revealed that the overall quality was influenced by the time spent using external resources and that, in HT, the overall error score was lower when the participants consulted external resources for a longer period of time (Daems et al., 2016). In this specific experiment, it seems that time and quality were in fact a trade-off. However, it is still unknown at this point whether this is the case with HT without external resources and/or in different language pairs.

The present study attempts to further elucidate the relationship between production time and translation quality using English-Japanese translation. The research question is: Can we predict the quality of translation based on characteristics of the ST and of individual translators? Here, the quality of translation is operationalized as number of errors, which has been correlated with several process metrics used as indicators of cognitive effort (Vanroy, 2021). A statistical method called zero-inflated generalized linear mixed models (ZIGLMMs) will be utilized, which nicely handles count data skewed by a large number zeros. By doing so, this study aims to identify which characteristics of a ST or a given translator potentially influence translation quality and efficiency.

In the following, Section 2 contains a description of the data; Section 3, the results of statistical analyses. In Section 4, the overall result will be discussed along with some findings from Ogawa (2021), where production duration was predicted by text and translator characteristics, in order to gain a better understanding of the relationship between ST and translator

[1]CRITT TPR-DB stands for Center for Research and Innovation in Translation and Translation Technology Translation Process Research Database. Behavioral and textual data from translation experiments is publicly available, and a list of publications utilizing this database is accessible at https://sites.google.com/site/centretranslationinnovation/tpr-db-publications?authuser=0.

characteristics and translation quality and efficiency.

2 Data and Methodology

The data used here was originally extracted from the ENJA15 project from the CRITT TPR-DB, in which 39 participants translated two out of six STs from scratch. In the present study, there were approximately 13 different translations for each ST.[2] The ".sg tables" from the CRITT TPR-DB were utilized, where the participants' textual and behavioral (i.e., typing and gaze) data is organized in a way that researchers can analyze it at the segment (i.e., sentence) level.

Errors were manually annotated and counted.[3] In doing so, although the unit of analysis was at the segment level, ST and TT did not necessarily have segment-level equivalence. In fact, some translators did divid one ST segment into two TT segments or combine two ST segments into one TT segment. The number of errors was approximated by the number of content words (i.e., nouns, verbs excluding auxiliary verbs, adjectives, and subordinating conjunctions) in the alignment group on the ST side. For example, a participant translated "was imprisoned" as 逮捕_さ_れ_まし_た (literally "was arrested"). This Japanese translation was morphologically analyzed and divided, as marked by underscores, into five tokens, and yet was aligned to "was imprisoned" as a group. In this case, there was only one content word on the ST side of this alignment group, and therefore, only one error was counted despite multiple TT tokens. This method of counting errors roughly but consistently quantified the severity of errors without judging them subjectively and dichotomously (e.g., minor versus critical).

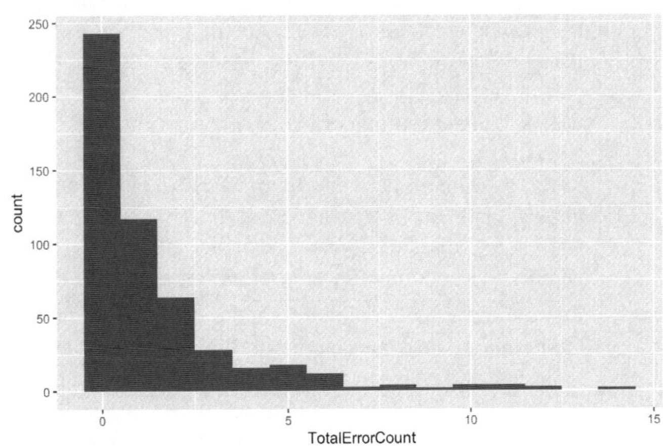

Figure 1: Distribution of TotalErrorCount

The resulting variable, named TotalErrorCount, ranged from 0 to 14 errors. 243 out of 520 segments had zero errors, and 117 segments only had one. As Figure 1 shows, the data was zero-inflated and overdispersed (i.e., the variance is greater than the mean). ZIGLMMs were utilized to handle this skewed data, which have two separate parts. The first part is a count model, which can be interpreted in the same manner as general linear mixed effect models. The count model explains what increases the number of errors. The other part is called a zero-inflated (ZI) model, whose interpretation is equivalent to a logistic regression. It calculates the

[2]See Ogawa (2021) for a more detailed description of the data analyzed.

[3]The errors were originally classified into four categories (i.e., mistranslation, cohesion, word order, and spelling), whose criteria are described in detail in Ogawa (2021). It turned out that approximately 84% of the errors were identified as mistranslation. In this present study, only the number of errors is discussed.

chance of contributing to excessive or structural zeros among all the zeros in the data. In this case, the ZI model tells us what affects the probability that a segment will have zero errors.

For this statistical analysis, packages called glmmTMB (Brooks et al., 2017) and DHARMa (Hartig, 2022) were used in RStudio (RStudio Team, 2022). A variable called Text, which identifies the six STs in CRITT TPR-DB, was used as a random effect for both count and ZI models. A backward step-wise selection method was adopted to build models; that is, a model was created with all the ST characteristics included in fixed effects, and one independent variable was removed at a time until all the fixed effects in the model were statistically significant ($p < 0.05$). Another set of models was created for translator characteristics in the same manner. The two different types of characteristics (ST and translator) were not combined in a single model so that the methodology would be identical to that of Ogawa (2021). The following is a sample model:

```
model <- glmmTMB(TotalErrorCount ~ 1 + fixed1 + fixed2 + (1|Text),
                 zi=~ fixed2 + (1|Text), data=df, family="nbinom1")
```

The independent variables tested in this study are described in Table 1 (see Ogawa 2021 for more detailed explanations of each variable). The first four are ST characteristics, and the last five are translator characteristics. Categorical variables are Figurative (3 levels), L1 (2 levels), InitialOrientation (4 levels), and EndRevision (3 levels). The rest are numeric variables.

Figurative	Refers to how many figurative expressions a segment contains.[4]
Ddepth	Refers to syntactic complexity of a segment. It counts the number of layers underneath the surface structure, processed by Berkeley Neural Parser (Kitaev et al., 2019; Kitaev and Klein, 2018). Higher values indicate greater syntactic complexity.
LWRatio	Refers to the proportion of words, per segment, that are longer than seven letters.
PROB1Norm	Refers to segment-level word frequency based on a log10 probability of a monogram ST word frequency calculated using the BNC corpus as a reference (Carl et al., 2016). The higher the value is, the greater the number of less common words a translator encounters in a segment.
Training	Indicates how many years of formal translation training a participant had.
Experience	Indicates how many years of translation experience a participant had.
L1	Indicates the participants' first language, either Japanese or English.
Initial Orientation	Categorizes sessions into four groups depending on how long the participant read the ST before starting to produce their translation (see Dragsted and Carl, 2013): Head-starters (who immediately started typing), Quick-planners (who read the first few ST sentences before typing), Scanners (who quickly scanned through the ST), and Systemic-planners (who read the entire ST).
EndRevision	Classifies sessions into three categories depending on how much time the participant spent re-reading the ST or TT after completing a draft: Long (more than 25% of the session duration was used for revision), Short (less than 25% of the session duration was used), and None (end revision was not conducted).

Table 1: Descriptions of ST/Translator Characteristics Used as Independent Variables

[4]This annotation has been revised and is therefore different from the annotation employed in Ogawa (2021), in which Figurative was a dichotomous annotation referring to whether a segment contains a metaphoric expression.

3 Results

3.1 Errors and ST Characteristics

The best model for estimating the number of errors from ST characteristics included Ddepth and LWRatio in the count model and LWRatio in the ZI model, and is summarized in Table 2.[5] The count model portion indicates that Ddepth and LWRatio positively impacted the TotalErrorCount. That is, the more syntactically complex the segment was and the greater number of long words the segment had, the greater number of errors the segment contained. Figure 2 visualizes a prediction based on this result, which shows that the predicted number of errors increases as Ddepth increases.[6] This tendency is maintained across different LWRatio values, and a greater number of errors are expected when LWRatio is higher.

	TotalErrorCount			
Predictors	*Estimate*	*Std. Error*	*z value*	*p*
Count Model				
(Intercept)	-0.68	0.24	-2.80	**0.005**
Ddepth	0.08	0.01	6.69	**<0.001**
LWRatio	1.68	0.75	2.25	**0.025**
Zero-Inflated Model				
(Intercept)	-4.94	1.48	-3.34	**0.001**
LWRatio	10.78	3.90	2.76	**0.006**
Random Effects				
σ^2	0.86			
$\tau_{00\ Text}$	0.10			
ICC	0.11			
N_{Text}	6			
Observations	520			
Marginal R^2 / Conditional R^2	0.137 / 0.229			

Table 2: Model Summary for ST Characteristics

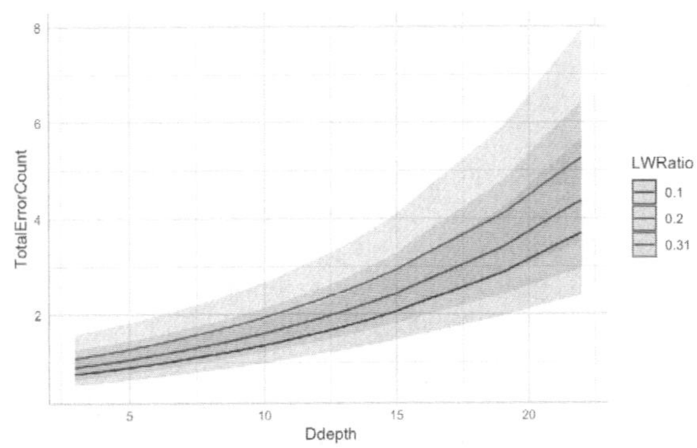

Figure 2: Predicted Number of Errors based on ST Characteristics

The middle section of Table 2 ("Zero-Inflated Model"), which should be interpreted as logistic regression, shows that LWRatio had a significant effect on excessive zeros. The positive estimate value, which is a log odds, indicates that it was more likely for a segment to be a member of excessive zeros as LWR increased. That is, when LWRatio was higher, a segment was more likely to contain zero errors. Converting the log odds to a probability (i.e., the exponential of the log-odds divided by the exponential of the log-odds plus one) suggests that a one-unit increase in LWRatio increases the chance of excessive zeros by 99%.

This is a puzzling result. How can LWRatio increase the number of errors while also increasing the chance of having zero errors with such a high probability? It might be because many of the segments with high LWRatio values contain zero errors. As Figure 3 illustrates, the segments with high (> 0.4) LWRatio only exist in Text 5, where the number of errors is relatively low. The two segments at the high end of LWRatio mostly contain zero errors, as

[5]The model summary tables in this study were produced using the *sjPlot* package (Lüdecke, 2021).

[6]The visualizations of predicted number of errors were produced using the *ggeffects* package (Lüdecke, 2018).

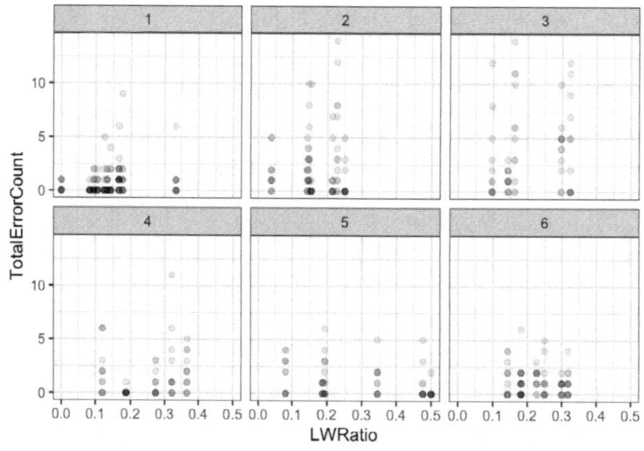

Figure 3: Distribution of LWRatio and TotalErrorCount in each ST

indicated by the dark dots. Also, the result might have been influenced by the fact that the range of LWRatio was too small (i.e., 0.0 to 0.5), which would make the change in log odds for a one-unit increase tremendous.

3.2 Errors and Translator Characteristics

The best model for estimating the number of errors based on translator characteristics included Experience, InitialOrientation and EndRevision in the count model and Training in the ZI model. Table 3 shows that, in the count model, Experience and EndRevision negatively influence the TotalErrorCount. That is, the participants who had more years of experience and spent more time on end revision made fewer errors. This is a somewhat expected (and pleasant) result.

As for InitialOrientation, Table 3 tells us that those who read STs before translating for at least some time (i.e., Quick-planners, Scanners, and Systemic-planners combined) made more errors than those who immediately started producing translation (i.e., Head-starters, the base level factor). This is a bit surprising given the fact that most errors in our dataset were mistranslation. Naively speaking, translators should be able to avoid making errors if they read the ST carefully, but this intuition was not supported by the result. Figure 4, which visualizes the predicted number of errors based on the count model, shows that Head-starters make the least number

	TotalErrorCount			
Predictors	*Estimate*	*Std. Error*	*z value*	*p*
Count Model				
(Intercept)	0.99	0.23	4.26	**<0.001**
Experience	-0.03	0.01	-3.77	**<0.001**
InitialOrientation [Quick-planner]	0.47	1.44	3.27	**0.001**
InitialOrientation [Scanner]	0.27	0.25	1.09	0.275
InitialOrientation [Systemic-planner]	0.35	0.17	2.09	**0.037**
EndRevision [Short]	-0.40	0.19	-2.13	**0.033**
EndRevision [Long]	-0.76	0.20	-3.74	**<0.001**
Zero-Inflated Model				
(Intercept)	-3.26	1.05	-3.11	**0.002**
Training	0.78	0.27	2.89	**0.004**
Random Effects				
σ^2	0.84			
$\tau_{00\ Text}$	0.17			
ICC	0.17			
N_{Text}	6			
Observations	492			
Marginal R^2 / Conditional R^2	0.145 / 0.287			

Table 3: Model Summary for Translator Characteristics

of errors, followed by Scanners, Quick-planners, and Systemic-planners in this order. Further examination revealed that the average years of experience per group decreased in the same order, although a statistically significant interaction effect was not found between InitialOrientation and Experience. It is also worth mentioning that InitialOrientation was annotated at the session level, not at the participant level, as some participants—regardless of their years of experience—spent very different amounts of time on ST reading across sessions. The result might have been different if the experiment had been conducted in a more ecologically valid situation, where the participants would exhibit their routine ST-reading habit.

Figure 4 also makes it clear that the number of errors decreases as years of experience increases, and that the Long group in EndRevision (i.e., participants who spent more than a quarter of session duration on end revision) produces fewer errors than the other two categories. Even translators who have zero experience seem to be able to greatly reduce the number of errors by spending more time on end revision. Jakobsen (2002) found that professional translators spent a greater proportion of time on end revision than student translators, and he presumed that professionals monitored and optimized their draft to achieve higher quality. The present study corroborates his observation, providing evidence that longer end revision leads to fewer errors.

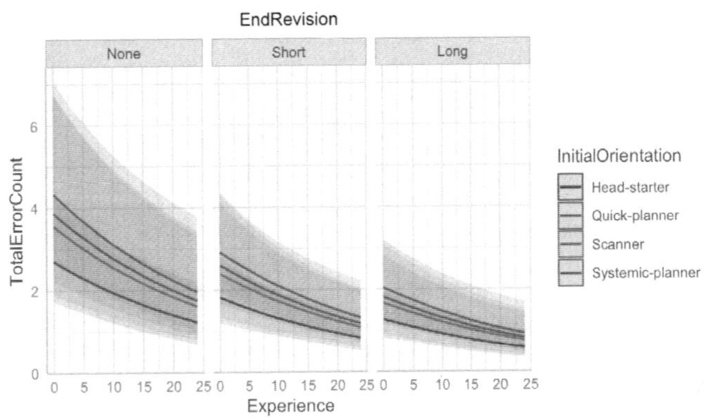

Figure 4: Predicted Number of Errors Based on Translator Characteristics

The ZI model in Table 3 indicates that Training had a positive impact. That is, the more training the participants had, the more likely a segment had zero errors. It is worth noting that Training was only significant in the ZI model. This suggests that years of training led to a significant difference in the production of error-free translation while it did not significantly reduce the number of errors. For example, a participant with one year of training is 69% (i.e., $exp(0.78)/(1 + exp(0.78))$ more likely to produce a translation with zero errors compared to a participant with no training, but when a participant with one year of training does make errors, the error count may or may not be lower than that of a translator with no training.

This result might suggest that, although training can help translators avoid making errors to a certain extent, having experience is crucial for overall translation quality. However, it may be necessary to consider what excessive zeros mean in the context of this specific translation experiment. In some studies, the concept is clear and easy to understand. For example, consider a situation where a researcher would like to know whether the number of visits to on-campus counseling services is influenced by the students' alcohol use. There would be many students who do not use counseling services at all, so the data would be zero-inflated. Among those zeros, students who are away from the campus or regularly see a counselor off campus would be members of excessive zeros because they are very unlikely to contribute to the count data. In our context, where participants translate English into Japanese without any external resources in an experimental setting, every participant can potentially make errors. Therefore, what excessive zeros are depends on how researchers interpret them.

Although this would greatly benefit from more discussion than we can achieve here, let us assume that excessive zeros represent an error-free translation produced when several factors coincide to create a "perfect situation," where translators make no errors. This is only a hypothetical situation, as we do not know what exactly creates such a "perfect situation" for translators. Nonetheless, it is reasonable to assume that translators with high expertise are unlikely to make errors when translating a segment that is easy for them.[7] Interpreted this way, the present study suggests that years of training increase the chances a translator will be in one of these "perfect situations" wherein they make zero errors. Perhaps Shreve (2009), who suggests that translators can increase their level of expertise by developing metacognitive skills, can provide us with a potential explanation. For instance, if the participants in our dataset in fact underwent some training that improved their metacognitive skills and as a result acquired heightened awareness of what kind of errors they tend to make, the results of the ZI model can be interpreted as supporting evidence that such training does have a positive impact on translation quality.

4 Discussion

The check marks in Table 4 indicate which characteristics produced a significant effect on TotalErrorCount in this study. Dur, on the right, refers to production duration (i.e., the time taken to translate a given segment, including pauses), and the results shown here are from Ogawa (2021). Dur is utilized to quantify time efficiency here, so that it will be clear which ST and translator characteristics influence translation quality and time efficiency in parallel.

	TotalErrorCount (count)	TotalErrorCount (ZI)	Dur
Figurative			
Ddepth	✔		
LWRatio	✔	✔	
PROB1Norm			✔
Training		✔	
Experience	✔		✔
L1			
InitialOrientation	✔		
EndRevision	✔		✔

Table 4: Statistically Significant Characteristics

Figurative and L1 were not significant in any models. Figurative expressions have been discussed and identified as a source of translation difficulty (e.g., Schäffner, 2004; Sjørup, 2008). A preliminary analysis on TotalErrorCount indeed indicated that Figurative produced a significant result in the count model, though only if it was the sole fixed effect in a model. Using the backward step-wise selection method may have lowered the explanatory power of Figurative when other independent variables were involved in a model. This might also be true for L1, which showed a significant result in the ZI model in a single fixed-effect model.

There was no ST characteristic that significantly influenced both TotalErrorCount and Dur, but two translator characteristics (i.e., Experience and EndRevision) were important factors for both dependent variables. Ogawa (2021) revealed that Dur was negatively influenced by

[7]Note that ease/difficulty are necessarily subjective. A segment can be easy for a translator if it is embedded in a rich context in their familiar domain without any words that they do not know.

Experience and positively influenced by EndRevision. That is, more experienced translators translated faster, and participants who spent more time on end revision had longer production duration as a result.[8] Combined with the finding in the present study, it can be concluded that i) years of experience is a good predictor of translation quality and time efficiency and that ii) the time translators spend on end revision inevitably increases production duration but in return increases quality.

Dur was also significantly influenced by PROB1Norm; participants spent more time translating as they encountered a greater number of less familiar or less frequently used words. Of course, each individual has different linguistic knowledge, and PROB1Norm is a simplistic operationalization of word familiarity. That being said, if PROB1Norm truly impacts Dur but not TotalErrorCount, it might be the case that translators can improve time efficiency by further familiarizing themselves with the source language. Familiarization would particularly matter when it comes to different genres or domains, where words are used as terms with different meanings than when they are used in general texts.

Ddepth and LWRatio increased the error count while Experience and EndRevision decreased it, as discussed in the previous section. The former two are ST characteristics that are fairly easy to quantify. It is not clear at this point whether pre-editing STs in such a way that Ddepth and LWRatio values will be lower leads to higher-quality translation. These characteristics may nevertheless be used to compare different texts and/or caution translators about potential difficulty in advance. The effects of Experience and EndRevision were also straightforward. This evidence may encourage translators to gain more experience and keep in mind that the end revision phase is critical to translation quality even when translators feel the need to prioritize time.

It may be worth mentioning that no clear relationship was observed between EndRevision and Experience. Recall that, in InitialOrientation, the Head-starter group was expected to produce the least number of errors and that the Quick-planner group the most. This can be explained by the fact that these two groups had the highest and lowest average years of experience respectively. In contrast, the Short group in EndRevision had the highest average years of experience, followed by the Long and None groups in this order. Moreover, participants who did not spend any time reviewing their draft (i.e., the None group) were most prevalent in the Head-starter group, and none of them belonged to the Quick-planner group. Although there was no clear relationship between EndRevision and InitialOrientation in this study, previous research has found that Head-starters and Quick-planners tended to prefer online revisions (i.e., revising as they produce a TT) while Scanners and Systemic-planners carried out end revision (Dragsted and Carl 2013). Perhaps, TotalErrorCount may be better analyzed if participant revision preferences, including online revision as well as end revision, are taken into consideration.

5 Future Directions

This paper has revealed that some ST and translator characteristics significantly contribute to the number of errors per segment in English-Japanese from-scratch translation. Combined with findings from a previous study, evidence was found that translators' years of experience make a difference in terms of translation quality and time efficiency, and that the length of end revision has a positive effect on quality even though it may take some extra time. However, the examination of translators' initial orientation phase with a ST suggested that there may be a complex interplay between the length of end revision and translator style (i.e., translator preferences for revisions and initial ST reading). This should be further scrutinized in future research.

[8]Note that EndRevision was defined by gaze data, not by typing activity. However, the fact that Dur was positively influenced by EndRevision may suggest that many of the participants who conducted end revision ended up making changes to their original draft.

This study was limited to English-Japanese translation, and hence, the result should be corroborated by similar studies using other languages. In doing so, methodology needs to be discussed in two respects. Firstly, the way of quantifying translation quality is of utmost importance since it can produce very different results. Error count is relatively easy to use as a quantification of translation quality but fails to recognize fine-grained differences in quality (e.g., it does not distinguish excellent from adequate quality). Some researchers have tried evaluating the quality of HT using metrics primarily used for machine translation (MT) output, such as BLEU (e.g., Carl and Buch-Kromann, 2010), and produced interesting results. At the same time, however, research has found that those metrics cannot fully capture errors in HT because HT errors are different from MT errors (Specia and Shah, 2014). Translation evaluation methods call for further discussions in TPR.

Even if the number of errors is used as a primary measure of translation quality, multiple evaluators and calculations of inter-rater reliability may need to be considered. Our study was limited to errors annotated by a single researcher, which admittedly is the biggest weakness of this paper. Furthermore, there may be a better way of counting errors. The method utilized (see Section 2) seems justifiable since it allows us to quantify errors regardless of the target language and to compare different studies in the CRITT TPR-DB. However, it does require significant manual work and may not be viable when multiple evaluators are involved.

The other methodological factor that demands attention is the use of ZIGLMMs. This is a fine-tuned statistical method that can deal with zero-inflated count data, but the interpretation of ZI models requires more discussion in TPR. Some researchers may find it implausible to assume excessive zeros in conducting this line of analysis.

Since many researchers in TPR use linear mixed effect models, it might be time for us to discuss what is considered a good model in our discipline. In this paper, the R^2 of the best model was 0.29, which means that roughly 30% of the total variance was explained by the model. This seems to be satisfactory as much smaller numbers have been reported (e.g., Ogawa, 2021; Vanroy et al., 2021), while much greater values have been achieved as well (e.g., Heilmann and Llorca-Bofí, 2021). Of course, it is risky to solely rely on R^2 as if it were the only criteria that could be used to validate an analysis. Such a discussion will surely lead to the advancement of methodology in TPR.

References

Brooks, M. E., Kristensen, K., van Benthem, K. J., Magnusson, A., Berg, C. W., Nielsen, A., Skaug, H. J., Maechler, M., and Bolker, B. M. (2017). glmmTMB balances speed and flexibility among packages for zero-inflated generalized linear mixed modeling. *The R Journal*, 9(2):378–400.

Carl, M. and Buch-Kromann, M. (2010). Correlating translation product and translation process data of professional and student translators. In *Proceedings of the 14th Annual conference of the European Association for Machine Translation*, Saint Raphaël, France. European Association for Machine Translation.

Carl, M., Schaeffer, M., and Bangalore, S. (2016). The CRITT translation process research database. In *New directions in empirical translation process research*, pages 13–54. Springer.

Colina, S. (2009). Further evidence for a functionalist approach to translation quality evaluation. *Target. International Journal of Translation Studies*, 21(2):235–264.

Daems, J., Carl, M., Vandepitte, S., Hartsuiker, R., and Macken, L. (2016). The effectiveness of consulting external resources during translation and post-editing of general text types. In *New directions in empirical translation process research*, pages 111–133. Springer.

Daems, J., Macken, L., and Vandepitte, S. (2013). Quality as the sum of its parts: A two-step approach for the identification of translation problems and translation quality assessment for ht and mt+ pe. In *Proceedings of the 2nd Workshop on Post-editing Technology and Practice*.

Dragsted, B. (2005). Segmentation in translation: Differences across levels of expertise and difficulty. *Target-international Journal of Translation Studies*, 17(1):49–70.

Dragsted, B. and Carl, M. (2013). Towards a classification of translation styles based on eye-tracking and key-logging data. *Journal of Writing Research*, 5(1):133–157.

Fields, P., Hague, D. R., Koby, G. S., Lommel, A., and Melby, A. (2014). What is quality? A management discipline and the translation industry get acquainted. *Revista Tradumàtica: tecnologies de la traducció*, 12:404–412.

Garvin, D. A. (1984). What does product-quality really mean. *Sloan management review*, 25:25–43.

Germann, U. (2008). Yawat: Yet another word alignment tool. In *Proceedings of the 46th Annual Meeting of the Association for Computational Linguistics on Human Language Technologies: Demo Session*, pages 20–23.

Hartig, F. (2022). *DHARMa: Residual Diagnostics for Hierarchical (Multi-Level / Mixed) Regression Models*. R package version 0.4.5.

Heilmann, A. and Llorca-Boff́í, C. (2021). Analyzing the effects of lexical cognates on translation properties: A multivariate product and process based approach. In *Explorations in Empirical Translation Process Research*, pages 203–229. Springer.

Hvelplund, K. T. (2011). *Allocation of cognitive resources in translation: An eye-tracking and key-logging study*. Doctoral thesis, Copenhagen Business School.

Jakobsen, A. L. (2002). Translation drafting by professional translators and by translation students. *Copenhagen studies in language*, 27:191–204.

Jakobsen, A. L. and Jensen, K. T. H. (2008). Eye movement behaviour across four different types of reading task. *Copenhagen studies in language*, 36:103–124.

Kitaev, N., Cao, S., and Klein, D. (2019). Multilingual constituency parsing with self-attention and pre-training. In *Proceedings of the 57th Annual Meeting of the Association for Computational Linguistics*, pages 3499–3505, Florence, Italy. Association for Computational Linguistics.

Kitaev, N. and Klein, D. (2018). Constituency parsing with a self-attentive encoder. In *Proceedings of the 56th Annual Meeting of the Association for Computational Linguistics (Volume 1: Long Papers)*, pages 2676–2686, Melbourne, Australia. Association for Computational Linguistics.

Kivilehto, M. and Salmi, L. (2017). Assessing assessment: The authorized translator's examination in finland. *Linguistica Antverpiensia, New Series–Themes in Translation Studies*, 16:57–70.

Lommel, A. (2018). Metrics for translation quality assessment: a case for standardising error typologies. In *Translation Quality Assessment*, pages 109–127. Springer.

Lüdecke, D. (2021). *sjPlot: Data Visualization for Statistics in Social Science*. R package version 2.8.7.

Lüdecke, D. (2018). ggeffects: Tidy data frames of marginal effects from regression models. *Journal of Open Source Software*, 3(26):772.

Mossop, B. (2014). *Revising and editing for translators*. Routledge.

Ogawa, H. (2021). *Difficulty in English-Japanese Translation: Cognitive Effort and Text/Translator Characteristics*. Doctoral thesis, Kent State University.

O'Brien, S. (2012). Towards a dynamic quality evaluation model for translation. *The Journal of Specialised Translation*, 17(1):55–77.

RStudio Team (2022). *RStudio: Integrated Development Environment for R*. RStudio, PBC, Boston, MA.

Schäffner, C. (2004). Metaphor and translation: Some implications of a cognitive approach. *Journal of pragmatics*, 36(7):1253–1269.

Sharmin, S., Spakov, O., Räihä, K.-J., and Lykke Jakobsen, A. (2008). Where on the screen do translation students look while translating, and for how long? *Copenhagen Studies in Language*, 36:31–51. Looking at Eyes: Eye-Tracking Studies of Reading and Translation Processing. (red.) Susanne Göpferich; Arnt Lykke Jakobsen; Inger M. Mees.

Shreve, G. M. (2009). Recipient-orientation and metacognition in the translation process. In Dimitriu, R. and Shlesinger, M., editors, *Translators and their readers: in homage to Eugene A. Nida*, pages 257–270. Les Editions du Hazard, Brussels.

Sjørup, A. C. (2008). Metaphor comprehension in translation: Methodological issues in a pilot study. *Copenhagen studies in language*, 36:53–77.

Specia, L. and Shah, K. (2014). Predicting human translation quality. In *Proceedings of the 11th Conference of the Association for Machine Translation in the Americas: MT Researchers Track*, pages 288–300.

Vanroy, B. (2021). *Syntactic Difficulties in Translation*. Doctoral thesis, Ghent University.

Vanroy, B., Schaeffer, M., and Macken, L. (2021). Comparing the effect of product-based metrics on the translation process. *Frontiers in Psychology*, 12.

The impact of translation competence on error recognition of neural MT

Moritz J. Schaeffer mschaeffer@uni-mainz.de
TRA&CO, University of Mainz, Germersheim, 76726, Germany

Abstract

Schaeffer et al. (2019) studied whether translation student's error recognition processes differed from those in professional translators. The stimuli consisted of complete texts, which contained errors of five kinds, following Mertin's (2006) error typology. Translation students and professionals saw translations which contained errors produced by human translators and which had to be revised. Vardaro et al (2019) followed the same logic, but first determined the frequency of error types produced by the EU commission's NMT system and then presented single sentences containing errors based on the MQM typology. Participants in Vardaro et al (2019) were professional translators employed by the EU. For the current purpose, we present the results from a comparison between those 30 professionals in Vardaro et al (2019) and a group of 30 translation students. We presented the same materials as in Vardaro et al (2019) and tracked participants' eye movements and keystrokes. Results show that translation competence interacts with how errors are recognized and corrected during post-editing. We discuss the results of this study in relation to current models of the translation process by contrasting the predictions these make with the evidence from our study.

1. Introduction

Translation competence has long been a more or less central issue in Translation Studies (e.g., Campbell, 1991; PACTE, 2003; Göpferich, 2009; Malmkjaer, 2009; Kiraly, 2013). In order to draw conclusions regarding what constitutes expert behaviour during translation and in order to eventually be in a position to model translation competence a number of studies have compared behaviour during translation by recruiting participants with different degrees of competence or expertise (e.g., Jakobsen, 2002; Rothe-Neves, 2003; Jensen & Pavlović, 2009; Dragsted, 2010; Carl et al, 2016; Daems et al, 2017). However, participant groups are typically formed in a binary fashion (e.g., students versus professionals), are created adhoc or in a qualitative manner. Few validated instruments which would make it possible to systematically compare different groups of participants beyond adhoc or qualitative categorization. The tool advanced by the PACTE group (Orozco & Hurtado Albir, 2002), e.g., offers hardly any numerical items, which makes quantitative analyses impossible or difficult, and the multiple-choice questions used to differentiate groups include very few response options, thus offering a rather limited coverage of what is to be modelled, i.e., translation competence. It is, in addition, difficult to generalize any findings in relation to this tool, given that two large parts consist in a translation and problem/error analysis task confined to an English text. Finally, PACTE provide scant statistical details about its external validation protocol.

The Translation and Interpreting Competence Questionaire (TICQ) presented by Schaeffer et al (2020) addresses a number of these issues. The TICQ establishes a gold-standard instrument for the systematic assessment of translation and interpreting competence and has been statistically demonstrated to robustly discriminate among participants with null, incipient, and professional experience. The predictive power of the questionnaire was tested with a discriminant function and results showed (Schaeffer et al 2020: 99) that this function could differentiate between innocent bilinguals, translation students and professional translators with a high degree of accuracy (70-84%).

2. Predictive power of the TICQ

While it has been shown that the TICQ successfully distinguishes between groups with different degrees of training and/or experience in the trade (Schaeffer et al 2020), the discriminant function used to do so models these differences in a continuous two-dimensional space. It therefore does justice to the fact that competence is highly unlikely to be categorical and much more likely to be better modelled on a continuous scale. While the ability to discriminate between groups of participants is useful and important, the purpose of the present paper is to test to what extent the coefficients within the discriminant functions used in Schaeffer et al (2020) are predictive of behaviour during translation.

The current study investigates how errors in translations produced by the neural machine translation (NMT) system employed by the Directorate General of Translation (DGT) of the European Comission are recognized and corrected by two groups of participants: professional translators working in-house at the DGT and translation students studyng at the University of Mainz. Both groups of participants filled in the TICQ, coeffcients for each participant were calculated on the basis of the discriminant function as described in Schaeffer et al (2020) and used to predict error recognition processes during post-editing.

3. Modelling translation competence

Schaeffer and Carl (2017) show that phrase based statistical machine translation systems (PBSMT) and human translators deal with translation ambiguity in a similar manner. Training of such a system involves creating expectations about possible a target texts given a source text. Schaeffer and Carl (2017) show that uncertainty as modeled in PBSMT systems is not unlike the uncertainty as moddeled by human translators – as measured by how the degree of uncertainty about possible target texts affects behaviour during translation: the greater the uncertainty of either human or machine, the longer the production durations. Carl (2021) shows that semantic vector space-based models encode small semantic discrepancies across languages such that they are predictive of behaviour during translation. Broadly, the larger the distances in vector space, the longer it takes human translators to process a translation. It is well known that the predictability of upcoming text has a large and very reliable effect on processing during reading (e.g., Smith and Levy, 2013). Whether phrase based statistical or vector space models of translation are more representative of how humans predict, produce and evaluate translations is an interesting question in itself, however, it is beyond doubt that there are large individual differences as to what kind of and how these expectations interact with how text is processed during translation – age, age of acquisition, expertise in a certain area, geographical factors and many others are likely to all affect how a much more fundamental statistical property of words, i.e. word form frequency, is predictive of reading behaviour (e.g., Chen et al, 2018). In other words, a bilingual person's expectations and associated uncertainty regarding translation is likely to differ substantially from a professional translator's expectations and associated uncertainty. Errors in existing text contravene expectations and how and when errors are recognized as contravening expectations and how and when errors are corrected is indicative of, well, the nature of those expectations, i.e., of the model of translation operating inside a particular (group of) human bilingual(s).

3.1. The current study: participants

Two groups of 30 participants each took part in the study. The group of professional translators were employed by the DGT and the students of translation were inscribed at the University of Mainz. Table 1 below shows the biographic data for student and professional participants. About half of the student participants were early bilinguals (age of acquisition of L2 before the age of 7), while this was the case for only 12% of the professionals. Language use was relatively balanced in both participant groups and professionals rated their own competence in L1, L2 and L3 higher (on a scale of 0 to 100).

	Students		Professionals	
	mean	sd	mean	sd
Age	21.6	(3.0)	46.0	(9.7)
Age at which L2 learning started	7.2	(2.6)	10.3	(3.0)
Number of years learning L2	13.5	(4.4)	12.0	(8.0)
Hours per week reading in L1	7.6	(5.1)	14.8	(11.3)
Hours per week reading in L2	5.9	(4.5)	16.0	(14.4)
Hours per week consuption of L1 Audio	5.0	(6.2)	2.6	(3.7)
Hours per week consuption of L2 Audio	2.7	(3.6)	2.5	(4.1)
Hours per week consuption of L1 AV material	6.1	(7.9)	5.3	(5.2)
Hours per week consuption of L2 AV material	6.0	(5.4)	3.8	(5.7)
Age at which L3 learning started	11.6	(4.0)	13.9	(5.4)
Number of years learning L3	8.3	(5.9)	9.7	(7.6)
Subjective Competence L1 (scale 0 – 100)	89.7	(8.2)	96.6	(3.4)
Subjective Competence L2 (scale 0 – 100)	76.8	(9.6)	82.6	(10.9)
Subjective Active Competence L3 (scale 0 – 100)	57.7	(19.8)	75.6	(12.4)
Subjective Passive Competence L3 (scale 0 – 100)	68.2	(17.8)	86.1	(7.8)
Early bilinguals (age of acquisition < 7 years of age) %	47%		12%	

Tabel 1: Biographic data for participants

Figure 1 visualises the scoring of participants according to the discriminant functions (F1z and F2z) as proposed by Schaeffer et al (2020). A reference line at the median for F1z has been introduced.

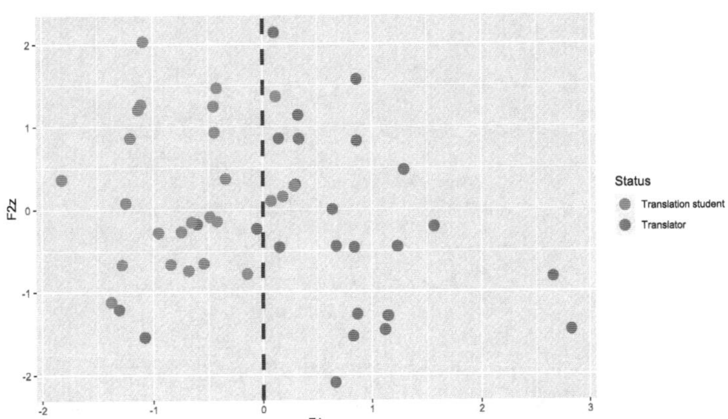

Figure 1: Visualization of scoring according to discriminant functions (Schaeffer et al 2020)

The reference line at the median for function F1z neatly separates participants into the two respective groups with a small number of outliers on each side of the divide.

3.2. Materials and task

The materials are identical to the ones used in Vardaro et al (2019). For a detailed description please consult Vardaro et al (2019). Suffice to say that participants saw single sentences which had been translated by the NMT engine as used at the DGT in 2019 and which had been postedited by in-house translators at the DGT. On the basis of a comparison between the raw NMT and the postedited texts, errors were identified. The sentences which participants saw either contained only one error or none. Each participant always only saw one version of each sentence (with or without error). Participants were asked to correct any mistakes they found nd were told that these had been produced by the in-house NMT of the DGT. In total, participants saw 81 sentences. No time restrictions were given.

3.3. Data gathering method

The sessions were recorded using the non-invasive eye-tracking device SMI RED250Mobile (250 Hz) and the eye-tracking and key-logging tool Translog-II (Carl 2012).

3.4. Data analysis

The statistical analysis with linear mixed-effect regression models (LMER) was carried out in R (R Core Team 2022), using the package lme4 (Bates et al, 2015). The package lmerTest (Kuznetsova et al, 2017) was used to calculate standard errors, effect sizes, and significance values. The effects of the models were visualized in plots for a better interpretation of each model by applying the effects package (Fox and Weisberg, 2019). Residuals outliers (> |2.5| SD) were excluded from the final model. To test for skewness and kurtosis, the package moments (Komsta and Novomestky, 2015) was used. After exclusion of residual outliers, skewness was below |2| and kurtosis below 7, meeting assumpptions of normality (Kim 2013).

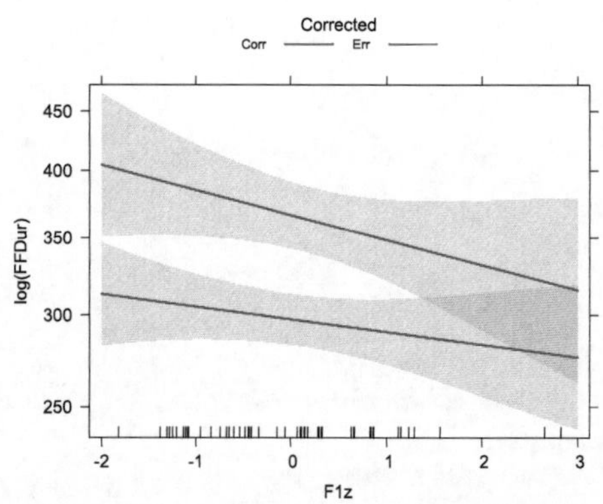

Figure 2: Effect of the presence of an error (Err) on first fixation durations. Errors are recognized during a first fixation, difference between Err and Corr (correct token). However, this effect does not interact with the competence score F1z (on the basis of the TICQ)

3.5. Results

Here, we report two models: We assume that if a token which we considered to be an error was corrected, it must have been recognized as such. The presence of an error did have an effect on first fixation durations ($p < .001$), but this early error recognition effect did not interact significantly ($p > .05$) with the F1z score derived from the TICQ (see above). In other words, irrespective of the participants' degree of translation competence, the time needed to recognize an error remained constant.

The second model traces the interaction between the early error recognition processes and the later stages of the postediting process, i.e., the eye-key span (Dragsted, 2010). The eye-key span (EKS) measures the time between a first visual contact with an error token and the timestamp of the first keystroke which contributed to the correction of this error token. It is reasonable to interpret the duration of the EKS in the following way: The longer the EKS, the more uncertain is the translator regarding the correction of an error that was recognized during a first fixation duration. In other words, the recognition processes taking place during a first fixation duration are likely to recruit largely automatic processes which pitch actual textual material against expectations regarding upcoming text. However, the processes which lead to a correction of the error token are likely to involve deliberations and monitoring processes which are less likely to be automatic. The model we report here, tested a twoway interaction between log-transformed first fixtion duration and the F1z score reported above, the dependent variable being the EKS. This twoway interaction was significant ($p < .01$).

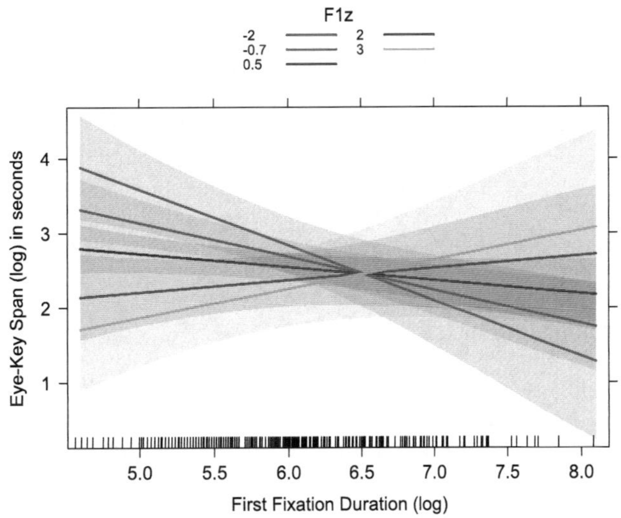

Figure 3: Interaction between log-transformed first fixation duration and F1z score for the Eye-key span.

The interaction was such that for participants with a higher F1z score the log-transformed first fixation duration had a positive effect on the EKS, which for those with a lower F1z score, the opposite was the case. If the error signal in the largely automatic processes was weak (short first fixation duration), for the more competent participants, this resulted in a short EKS. If, however, the error signal in the largely automatic processes was strong (long first fixation duration), for the more competent participants, this resulted in a long EKS. In other words, participants with a higher F1z score blindly trusted a weak error signal: they corrected the error quickly, while a srong error signal resulted in effortful revision of the output from the early processes before a correction could be carried out. For participants with a lower F1z score, the opposite was the case. Those with less translation competence trusted the largely automatic early error recognition processes blindly only if the error signal was strong (long first fixation durations). The longer the first fixation duration, the shorter the EKS. However, if the error signal from the early processes was weak, they required effortful and lengthy revision of the output from the early processes.

4. Discussion

The present paper shows that a score based on the TICQ (Schaeffer et al 2020) is predictive of error recognition processes in a group of participants with differing degrees of translation competence. The score presented here is on a continuous scale, derived irrespective of a particular language (combination), it can discriminate between differing degrees of translation competence. It does so, in particular, for the interaction between early error recognition and late error correction processes. As such, it is in line with e.g., the model proposed by Schaeffer and Carl (2013), which proposed that output from early, automatic processes is evaluated by later processes. It is the interaction between the early and late stages of error recognition and correction which is carried out differently by participants with differing degrees of translation competence. The scores based on the TICQ are promising not only because they may serve to directly compare participants with different biographies and stages of professional development, but also because they can be predictive of complex behavioural patterns which are relevant to aspiring practicing professional translators, on the one hand, and on the other hand, they may be used to further refine models of the translation process.

References

Bates, D. *et al.* (2015) 'Fitting Linear Mixed-Effects Models Using lme4', *Journal of Statistical Software*, 67(1), pp. 1–48. Available at: https://doi.org/10.18637/jss.v067.i01.

Campbell, S.J. (1991) 'Towards a Model of Translation Competence', *Meta: Journal des traducteurs*, 36(2–3), p. 329. Available at: https://doi.org/10.7202/002190ar.

Carl, M. (2012) 'Translog-II : a Program for Recording User Activity Data for Empirical Reading and Writing Research', in *The Eighth International Conference on Language Resources and Evaluation. 21-27 May 2012, Istanbul, Tyrkiet*. Department of International Language Studies and Computational Linguistics, pp. 2–6.

Carl, M., Aizawa, A. and Yamada, M. (2016) 'English-to-Japanese Translation vs . Dictation vs . Post-editing : Comparing Translation Modes in a Multilingual Setting', in N. Calzolari et al. (eds) *The LREC 2016 Proceedings: Tenth International Conference on Language Resources and Evaluation*. Portorož: ELRA, pp. 4024–4031.

Carl, M. and Schaeffer, M.J. (2017) 'Why Translation Is Difficult : A Corpus-Based Study of Non-Literality in Post-Editing and From-Scratch Translation', *Hermes - Journal of Language and Communication Studies*, (56), pp. 43–57.

Chen, X., Dong, Y. and Yu, X. (2018) 'On the predictive validity of various corpus-based frequency norms in L2 English lexical processing', *Behavior Research Methods*, 50(1), pp. 1–25. Available at: https://doi.org/10.3758/s13428-017-1001-8.

Daems, J. *et al.* (2017) 'Translation Methods and Experience: A Comparative Analysis of Human Translation and Post-editing with Students and Professional Translators', *Meta*, 62(2), pp. 245–270. Available at: https://doi.org/10.7202/1041023ar.

Dragsted, B. (2010) 'Coordination of Reading and Writing Processes in Translation: An Eye on Unchartered Territory', in G.M. Shreve and E. Angelone (eds) *Translation and Cognition*. Amsterdam and Philadelphia: John Benjamins.

Fox, J. and Weisberg, S. (2019) *An R Companion to Applied Regression, 3rd Edition*. Thousand Oaks, CA. Available at: https://socialsciences.mcmaster.ca/jfox/Books/Companion/index.html.

Göpferich, S. (2009) 'Towards a Model of Translation Competence and its Acquisition: the Longitudinal Study TransComp', in S. Göpferich, A.L. Jakobsen, and I.M. Mees (eds) *Behind the Mind: Methods, Models and Results in Translation Process Research*. Copenhagen: Samfundslitteratur (Copenhagen Studies in Language 37), pp. 11–37.

Jakobsen, A.L. (2002) 'Translation drafting by professional translators and by translation students', in G. Hansen (ed.) *Empirical Translation Studies: process and product*. Copenhagen: Samfundslitteratur, pp. 191–204.

Jensen, K.T.H. and Pavlović, N. (2009) 'Eye tracking translation directionality', in A. Pym and A. Perekrestenko (eds) *Translation research projects 2*, pp. 93–109.

Kim, H.-Y. (2013) 'Statistical notes for clinical researchers: assessing normal distribution (2) using skewness and kurtosis', *Restorative Dentistry & Endodontics*, 38(1), p. 52. Available at: https://doi.org/10.5395/rde.2013.38.1.52.

Kiraly, D. (2013) 'Towards a View of Translators Competence as a Emergent Phenomenon: Thinking Outside the Box(es) in Translation Education', *New Prospects and Perspectives for Educating Language Mediators*, (January 2013), p. 197.

Komsta, L. and Novomestky, F. (2015) *moments: Moments, cumulants, skewness, kurtosis and related tests*. Available at: https://CRAN.R-project.org/package=moments.

Kuznetsova, A., Brockhoff, P.B. and Christensen, R.H.B. (2017) 'lmerTest Package: Tests in Linear Mixed Effects Models', *Journal of Statistical Software*, 82(13), pp. 1–26. Available at: https://doi.org/10.18637/jss.v082.i13.

Malmkjær, K. (2009) 'What is translational competence?', *Revue française de linguistique appliquée*, 14(1).

Orozco, M. and Hurtado Albir, A. (2002) 'Measuring Translation Competence Acquisition', *Meta*, 47(3), pp. 375–402. Available at: https://doi.org/10.7202/008022ar.

PACTE (2003) 'Building a Translation Competence Model', in F. Alves (ed.) *Triangulating Translation: Perspectives in Process Oriented Research*. Amsterdam and Philadelphia: John Benjamins, pp. 43–66. Available at: https://doi.org/10.1075/btl.45.06pac.

R Core Team (2022) *R: A Language and Environment for Statistical Computing*. Vienna, Austria: R Foundation for Statistical Computing. Available at: https://www.R-project.org/.

Rothe-Neves, R. (2003) 'The Influence of Working Memory Features on Some Formal Aspects of Translation Performance', in *Triangulating Translation: Perspectives in Process Oriented Research*. Amsterdam and Philadelphia: John Benjamins, pp. 97–119.

Schaeffer, M. *et al.* (2020) 'The Translation and Interpreting Competence Questionnaire: an online tool for research on translators and interpreters', *Perspectives*, 28(1), pp. 90–108. Available at: https://doi.org/10.1080/0907676X.2019.1629468.

Smith, N.J. and Levy, R. (2013) 'The effect of word predictability on reading time is logarithmic', *Cognition*, 128(3), pp. 302–319. Available at: https://doi.org/10.1016/j.cognition.2013.02.013.

Syntactic Cross and Reading Effort in English to Japanese Translation

Takanori Mizowaki 22wv006d@rikkyo.ac.jp
Graduate School of Intercultural Communication, Rikkyo University, Tokyo, 1718501, Japan
Haruka Ogawa ogawaha@earlham.edu
Department of Languages and Cultures, Earlham College, Richmond IN, 47374, USA
Masaru Yamada masaru.yamada@rikkyo.ac.jp
College of Intercultural Communication, Rikkyo University, Tokyo, 1718501, Japan

Abstract

In English to Japanese translation, a linear translation refers to a translation in which the word order of the source text is kept as unchanged as possible. Previous research suggests that linear translation reduces the cognitive effort for interpreters and translators compared to the non-linear case. In this study, we empirically tested whether this was also the case in a monolingual setting from the viewpoint of reception study. The difference between linear and non-linear translation was defined using Cross values, which quantify how much reordering was required in Japanese translation relative to an English source text. Reading effort was measured by the average total reading time on the target text. In a linear mixed-effects model analysis, variations in reading time per participant and text type were also considered random effects. The results revealed that the reading effort for the linear translation was smaller than that for the non-linear translation. In addition, the accuracy of text comprehension was also found to affect the reading time.

1. Introduction

Linear translation is a translation strategy utilized by translators to preserve the word order of the source text to the maximum possible extent. This strategy is commonly used among English-to-Japanese simultaneous interpreters. It helps reduce the interpreter's cognitive effort and prevents their working memory from overloading (Mizuno, 2005) especially because the syntactic structures of English and Japanese mirror each other (i.e., the basic word order of SOV [subject-object-verb] in Japanese contrasts with the SVO of English). When an original English speech in S<u>VO</u> is heard and interpreted into the target Japanese S<u>OV</u>, the interpreter needs to retain the V (verb = simple predicate) in working memory until translating the following O (object).

Linear translation strategy is also said to help not only interpreters but readers of written translation. Translated texts with the use of a linear translation strategy are said to help to understand better because they "do not disrupt the flow of thought of the source text (Anzai, 1995)" and retain the "information structure" of the source text (Mizuno, 2022; Naganuma et al., 2016). Consequently, they are also thought to reduce reading effort because of the simplified syntactic complexity of the target text (Table 1)[1]. For example, the part of source and target texts in square brackets in Table 1 are relative clauses. The source text contains an accusative noun, *a book*, which is the head of a relative clause that accompanies *that Mary read two years ago*. When this source text is translated into Japanese in a non-linear manner, the relative clause is usually placed before the accusative noun in the target rendition, as shown in the example of a non-linear translation. In this case, the main clause—*Tom bought the book*—is split into two parts by the inserted relative clause, and the head of the sentence (predicate) *buy* appears at the end of the target text; therefore, the reader of the target text has to retain more information (i.e., a larger number of "chunks" that makes up the relative clause) in their working memory, resulting in higher cognitive effort in reading. Therefore, non-linear translation is more difficult than linear translation for the reader, where the inserted relative clause does not hinder the main clause. The head of the sentence also appears as early as in the source text.

To the best of our knowledge, however, no empirical investigation of reception study for the reading effort of linear translations has been carried out. This study aims to test a hypothesis as to whether linear translation takes less cognitive effort in reading without the source text being presented than non-linear translation.

Source Text	Tom bought a book [that Mary read two years ago].
Non-Linear Translation	トムは [メアリーが2年前に読んだ] 本を買った。 Tom-Top [Mary-Nom two-years-ago-Temp read-Past] book-Acc buy-Past. Tomu-wa [mearii-ga ni-nen-mae-ni yon-da] hon-o kat-ta.
Back translation	Tom bought a book that Mary read two years ago.
Linear Translation	トムは本を買った。[メアリーが2年前に読んだ]ものだ。 Tom-Top book-Acc buy-Past. [Mary-Nom two-years-ago-Temp read-Past] thing is. Tomu-wa hon-o kat-ta. [Mearii-ga ninen-mae-ni yon-da] mono da.
Back translation	Tom bought a book. It is the one Mary read two years ago.

Table 1. Example of an English source text and a Japanese linear and non-linear translation

2. Related Works

In translation process research, the idea of Cross, which counts how many words in the source language must be skipped to produce the subsequent word in the target language, has been used to quantify differences in syntactic structure between the source text and target text (Carl et al., 2016). Cross value is a vital indicator to define linear and non-linear translation in this study.

Carl and Schaeffer (2017) analyzed the relationship between translation literality and translation effort. They use Cross to quantify the similarity of the syntactic structure of the source text and the target text. The researchers found that translation production time increased as the translation became less linear. Furthermore, Lacruz et al. (2018) investigated the interaction of the cognitive effort during translation with semantic and syntactic remoteness between the source and target language. They quantified the syntactic remoteness with the Cross and used the pause-word ratio (PWR) as a proxy for cognitive effort. This study also found a strong positive correlation between syntactic remoteness and cognitive effort in English to Japanese translations.

Despite the number of studies investigating the relationship between syntactic Cross and cognitive effort needed for translators, few studies have focused on translation readers' perception in terms of reading cognitive effort and compare the linear vs. non-linear translations. Some studies have briefly discussed cognitive effort in linear translation by exploring the related process of sight translation. The pilot experiment of Yamada and Naganuma (2019)—wherein

[1] The gloss used in this paper is as follows: Top=Topic, Nom=Nominative, Temp=Temporal, Acc=Accusative, Dat=Dative

translation process data collected for English to Japanese sight translation were compared by Cross value between linear and non-linear translation—found that the Cross value produced during sight translation was close to that of linear translation (Yamada & Naganuma, 2019, p. 98).

Hirose (2003) focused on prosodic structure and how it affects readers' selection of a particular reading from different options when reading a Japanese sentence containing relative clauses. That is, a sentence with high Cross value is more likely to produce a cause ambiguous reading, increasing reading effort. An example of syntactic ambiguity caused by the syntactic properties of Japanese is cited below (Hirose, 2003, p. 168).

(1) 森下が<u>新薬</u>を心から**信用した**友人達に
Mori'sita-ga <u>si'nyaku</u>-o kokoro'kara **sinyoosita** yuuji'ntati-ni
Morisita-Nom <u>new medicine</u>-Acc truly **trusted** friends-Dat

In example (1), the verb *si'nyoosita* (trusted) (bold) remains syntactically ambiguous until the reader sees *yuuji'ntati* (friends). Until then, other interpretations such as "Morishita truly trusted new medicine" are possible. Furthermore, the ambiguity of *si'nyaku* (new medicine) (underlined) is not resolved until the reader sees the predicate that follows *friends*.

(2) 森下が[新薬を心から信用した]友人達にとうとう会った。
Mori'sita-ga [si'nyaku-o kokoro'kara sinyoosita] yuuji'ntati-ni to'otoo a'tta.
Morisita-Nom new medicine-Acc truly trusted friends-Dat finally met

In (2), the predicate is a transitive verb *a'tta* (meet). In this case, syntactic ambiguity with the relative clause is determined as indicated by the square brackets.

Nakamura and Arai (2012) measured the effort in reading Japanese garden-path sentences using an eye tracker, showing that the cost of reanalyzing Japanese garden-path sentences is high and that the effort might reflect the degree of the reader's commitment to first-pass reading.

In sum, complex syntactic structures with high Cross values are likely to affect readers' cognitive effort, as non-linear translation likewise may be cognitively taxing; however, it is expected that linear translation may produce an opposite result.

3. Research Question and Experimental Settings

3.1. Research Question

This study is a reception study that examines whether translated texts using a linear translation strategy, resulted in smaller Cross value, will reduce reading effort, compared to the case where they are tasked with reading non-linear translation (with higher Cross value). To this end, we carried out an empirical experiment to collect data on reading effort from different readers. The experiment settings and our definition of reading are described below:

- Readers are people who routinely read Japanese texts, regardless of their native language.
- They read only the target text (i.e., the source text is not presented).
- They read silently, aiming to comprehend the content of the text.

The research question of this study is as follows:

Is the reading effort of linear translation lower than that of non-linear translation?

TO test the research question, we prepared linear and non-linear translations, asked 15 participants to read them, and collected the gaze data from reading them using an eye tracker.

3.2. Metrics to measure the reading effort

We prepared two types of translation for each source text: linear and non-linear. To determine the difference between the linear and non-linear translation, we used the Cross value and Cross rate proposed by Okamura and Yamada (2020). These metrics quantify differences in syntactic structure between source and target texts in a similar way as Cross in Carl et al. (2016); however, they are calculated in chunk units (minimum syntactic unit of meaning) rather than word units (for a detailed definition of chunks, see Okamura and Yamada, 2020).

We also drew on the concept of Normalized Total Reading Time on the Target Text (nTrtT; see Ogawa, 2021) to examine the cognitive effort of reading; however, we divided the reading time by the number of words[2] in the target text rather than the source text. A longer reading time suggests a higher cognitive effort. In our study, reading time is the total fixation duration captured by an eye tracker. The research question, therefore, can be paraphrased as follows: Is the nTrtT value (i.e., reading effort) of a target text with a small Cross value (i.e., linear translation) lower than that of a target text with a large Cross value (i.e., non-linear translation)?

3.3. Participants

We recruited participants who had completed three or more years of undergraduate study with relatively high command over both English and Japanese. A total of 15 participants joined the experiment: 10 native Japanese speakers and five native speakers of other languages, including English, Russian, Thai, and Spanish. Although we did not establish any standards to control the participants' English and Japanese language skills, the average TOEIC® Listening & Reading Test score was 814.09 only for those who responded to the post-experiment survey. Three of the native speakers of the other languages obtained Level 1 proficiency in the Japanese-Language Proficiency Test. Since variation in reading performance among the participants occurred in any case and was considered in the analysis, we considered it a reasonable profile of the participants.

3.4. Experimental Texts

The experimental texts were prepared in the following way. First, we collected general English online news articles that had already been translated into Japanese (approximately 150 characters, three to five sentences). For a particular sentence in the article, two versions of translation were prepared: linear and non-linear. The sentence with two types of translations is called an "experimental segment," which is targeted for analysis. No changes are added except for the target segment. The criteria for the experimental segment were as follows: 1) the number of chunks (Okamura & Yamada, 2020) must be at least seven, and 2) the segment must contain a restrictive relative clause (Mizuno, 2022).

For the experimental segment, two patterns of linear and non-linear translation were prepared by changing only the function words and the position of the content words. The criteria for linear translation were as follows:

[2] The word is the smallest unit in a sentence when it is separated by the Japanese morphological analysis tool, MeCab (Kudo et al., 2004).

1. The antecedent is translated first, followed by the restrictive relative clause.
2. Cross value and Cross rate are less than double those of non-linear translation.

The criteria for non-linear translation are as follows:

1. The restrictive relative clause is translated first, followed by the antecedent.
2. Cross value and Cross rate are more than double those of linear translation.

The linear and non-linear translations prepared by these criteria are distinguished in the analysis by the categories J for *junokuri* (linear translation) and G for *gyakuokuri* (non-linear translation). The variable name for this distinction is JvsG in this study.

Four sets of texts (articles) were prepared in the same manner. One of the four texts was used for practice and the other three (i.e., Texts 1, 3, and 5) for data collection. The variable that identifies these texts is named OriginalText.

3.5. Experimental Procedure

The experiment was conducted in the following steps.

1. Orient each participant to the experiment's flow and the text's outline displayed on the computer screen.
2. Calibrate and validate the eye tracker.
3. Present the target texts on the screen.
4. Conduct a comprehension test after each reading.

We used Translog-II (Carl, 2012b) to display the experimental texts in step 3. The order in which the texts were displayed was randomized for each participant. A simple comprehension test (two questions about the content) in Step 4 was conducted to secure the quality of each reading. It consisted of two correct/incorrect questions about the content of the texts (created with reference to Royer et al., (1987)). The test results were used in a statistical analysis as a three-level categorical variable (hereafter referred to as Test). *Zero* refers to no correct answer out of two questions, *Half* to one correct answer, and *Full* to two correct answers. The overall percentage of questions answered correctly was 83%. The data collected through these procedures was uploaded to the CRITT TPR-DB[3] (Carl et al., 2016). After aligning the source and target texts, the tables were generated for analysis (only the experimental segments were used for analysis).

4. Results and Discussion

4.1. Quantitative analysis using Linear Mixed-Effects Models

Figure 1 is a boxplot visualizing the differences in nTrtT for each participant. The part on the x-axis refers to the 15 participants. For example, the participant named P08 tends to spend more time reading the target segments than the other participants. In contrast, P05, P12, P13, and P15 read the target segments in a relatively short time. Thus, the reading time varies significantly among the participants, which should be considered in subsequent statistical analyses. Figure 2

[3] Translation Process Research Database of the Center for Research and Innovation in Translation and Translation Technology (https://sites.google.com/site/centretranslationinnovation/tpr-db)

is a boxplot showing nTrtT for each text, where the OriginalText on the x-axis refers to the text number (Texts 1, 3, and 5). This figure shows that reading time among the texts differs significantly.

These figures indicate that the participants and texts may affect the reading time of the linear and non-linear translations. In other words, since there is a considerable variation in the reading time depending on the participants, and the differences among the three experimental texts (e.g., the differences in topics in each article) affect the reading time (i.e., cognitive effort), it may be difficult to see whether the difference between the linear and non-linear translation affects the reading time. Based on these results, the following statistical analysis was conducted.

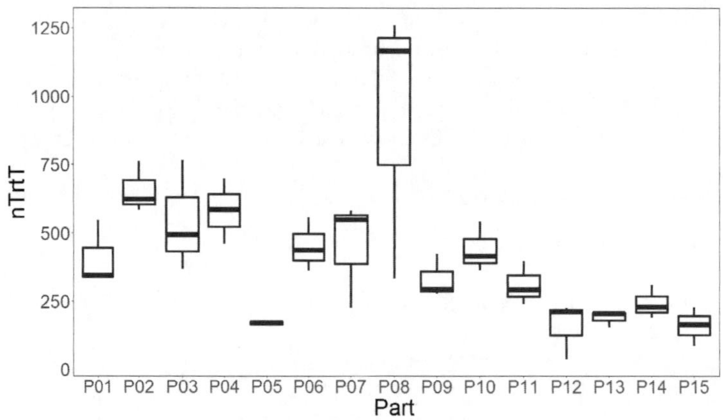

Figure 1. nTrtT for each participant

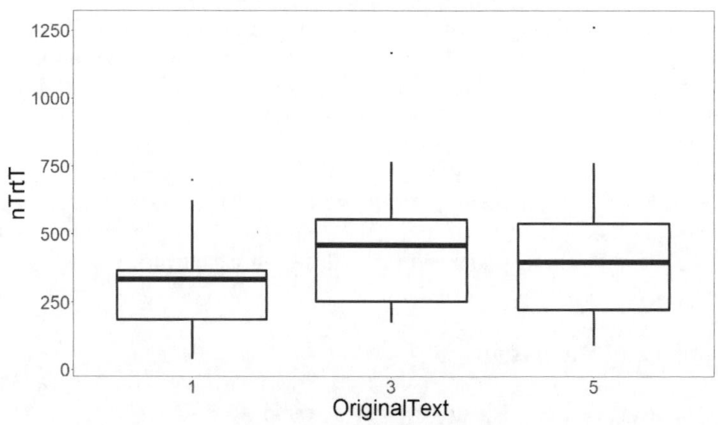

Figure 2. nTrtT for each text

We used linear mixed-effects models[4]; nTrtT was the outcome variable. In addition, two variables, Part (participants) and OriginalText (experimental texts), were included as random effects, which are reflected only in the intercept; this allows us to consider that the average

[4] Statistical analysis was performed on R (version 4.1.2 (R Core Team, 2021)) and RStudio. lme4 (Bates et al., 2015), lmerTest (Kuznetsova et al., 2017), sjPlot (Lüdecke, 2021), and ggplot2 (Wickham, 2016) were used.

reading time may vary depending on the individual participant and the text type. The predictors were selected from several candidates: Cross values, Cross rate, JvsG (difference between linear and non-linear translation), Test (results of comprehension tests), number of chunks, Japanese readability score, and Flesch-Kincaid Grade Level. We tried combinations of these predictors and selected the model with the lowest AIC.

	nTrtT			
Predictors	*Estimates*	*std. Error*	*CI*	*p*
(Intercept)	373.14	69.60	232.24 – 514.05	**<0.001**
JvsG [G]	101.59	40.93	18.74 – 184.44	**0.018**
Test [Half]	-29.81	53.33	-137.78 – 78.16	0.579
Test [Zero]	-303.99	83.93	-473.90 – -134.07	**0.001**
Random Effects				
σ^2	13753.54			
$\tau_{00\ Part}$	48673.89			
$\tau_{00\ OriginalText}$	1920.37			
ICC	0.79			
N_{Part}	15			
$N_{OriginalText}$	3			
Observations	45			
Marginal R^2 / Conditional R^2	0.125 / 0.813			

Table 2. Summary of JvsG + Test model

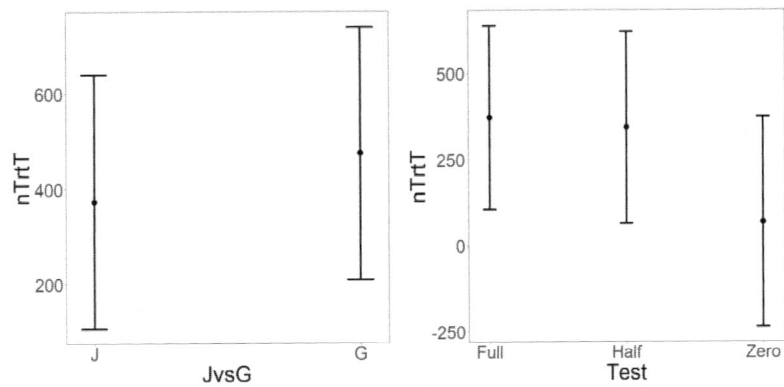

Figure 3. Plots of JvsG + Test model

Consequently, a model with JvsG and Test as predictors was selected. Table 2 summarizes the model, and we can discern two points from the top part of the table. First, the reading time for the non-linear translation was significantly longer than that of the linear translation for the participants who answered both questions correctly on the comprehension test. Second, among participants who read the linear translation, those who answered either one or both questions correctly on the comprehension test had significantly longer reading times than those who answered none correctly. The results of this model are plotted in Figure 3. The left plot shows that reading time tends to be shorter for the linear translation than for the non-linear translation. The right plot indicates that participants who performed better on the comprehension test (i.e., those who read and understood the text well) tended to spend more time reading the target text. These results suggest that linear translation requires less reading effort than non-linear translation.

The bottom part of Table 2 also indicates that random effects contribute significantly to this model. The intraclass correlation coefficient (ICC) shows that 79% of the variance is explained by the random variables, suggesting that using a linear mixed-effects model was appropriate. In addition, since Conditional R2 is large compared to Marginal R2, random effects contribute significantly to the model. Marginal R2 refers to the proportion of variance explained by the predictors (i.e., JvsG and Test), while Conditional R2 refers to the proportion of variance explained by these two predictors and two random variables (i.e., participants and text type).

4.2. Qualitative analysis using progression graphs

Since the statistics above show differences in reading cognitive effort between linear and non-linear translation, we created progression graphs visualizing reading processes involving regression or complex behaviors. Progression graphs enables analyzing translators' activity data. It represents the distribution of gaze activities over time (e.g., Carl, 2012a; Carl and Kay, 2011). As shown in Figure 4, the x-axis represents time progression, indicated by timestamps in ms, while the y-axis (on the right) represents Japanese target words. The target text begins at the bottom of the y-axis and ends at the top. Figure 4 shows excerpts from the readings of two participants (P10 and P15) who were reading the experimental segment of Text 1. The left plot shows P10 reading the linear translation, and the right plot shows P15 reading the non-linear translation. The black dots are fixations, and the black lines connecting them are saccades. Red lines across the graph indicate breaks of chunks (see Okamura and Yamada, 2021). In general, when the graph rises smoothly toward the right upper corner with small numbers of fluctuations, one can summarize that there is a lower degree of cognitive effort involved in the participant's reading.

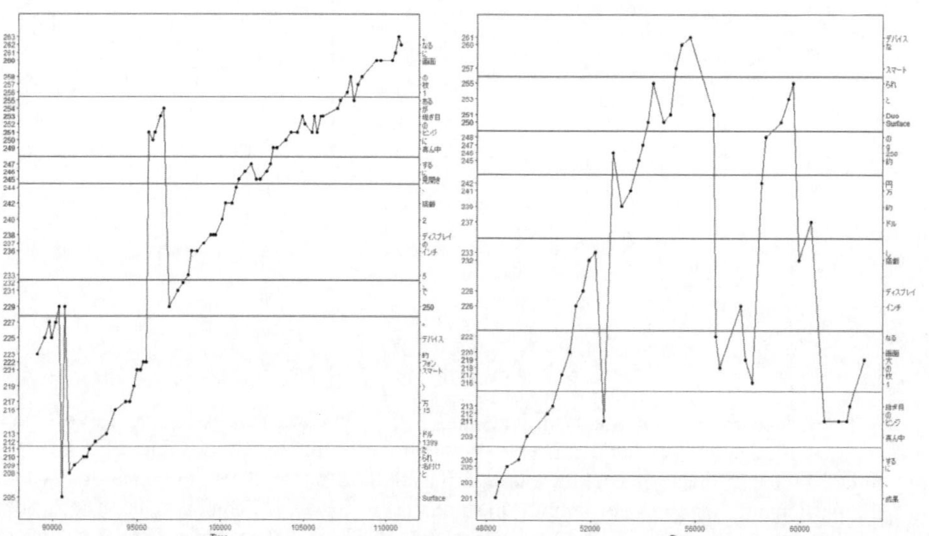

Figure 4. Progression graphs of P10 reading a linear translation (left) and P15 reading a non-linear translation (right)

P10 (left), reading a linear translation, reads the target text relatively progressively. In contrast, P15 (right), reading a non-linear translation, frequently re-read the previous part of the sentence across chunks.

In particular, in the non-linear translation (right), the participant seems to read the entire sentence once before 56,000 ms, and after 56,000 ms, the participant re-reads it by going back and forth between the parts of the sentence read once before. It is evident from these observations that the syntactic complexity of non-linear translation may require the reader to re-read the target text.

The relationship between progression graphs and linear translation needs further investigation because the difference observable in Figure 4 may be due to the idiosyncracies among participants.

5. Conclusion

This study investigated the relationship between linear translation and readers' cognitive effort. Linear translation in this study was defined as having a relatively low Cross value and Cross rate (Okamura & Yamada 2020). In a non-linear translation, the Cross value and Cross rate are relatively high. We prepared texts containing linear or non-linear translations and conducted reading experiments using an eye tracker to measure the readers' cognitive effort. Total reading time was used as a metric of cognitive effort. We then examined what factors influenced the reading time, including Cross value, Cross rate, JvsG, and the results of a comprehension test, while also considering uncontrollable factors due to the variation among participants and experimental texts. The results revealed that the type of translation (linear or non-linear) and the comprehension test results significantly impacted the reading time. In addition, qualitative analysis of the progression graphs suggested that non-linear translation is likely to be read more regressively than linear translation.

The research question is, "Is the reading effort of linear translation lower than that of non-linear translation?" The results of this study indicate that the reading effort of linear translation is lower than that of non-linear translation. Moreover, to explain the reading time used as a measure of effort in this study, it is necessary to consider the type of translation and also the comprehension of the text. This result is proof of our intuition that reading time is longer for those who read with a correct understanding of the text, but we realized the necessity of improving the ecological validity of the experiment by fully specifying the purpose of the reading for participants. Furthermore, some translation studies have shown that cognitive effort depends on the purpose of reading (Jakobsen & Jensen, 2008; Ruiz et al., 2008). Therefore, we would like to continue research to measure cognitive effort after encouraging reading with comprehension rather than just following the text.

One of the limitations of this study is the considerable variation in reading times across texts. As indicated by the bottom part of Table 2, even in the best model finally employed in this study, the random variables had higher explanatory power than the predictors. Although it is impossible to control the variation in participants' reading, the texts used in the experiments must be reconsidered. By collecting more data from more participants, we would like to continue investigating what contributes to the cognitive effort.

References

Anzai, T. (1995). *Eibun honyaku jutsu* [A technique of translating English sentences]. Chikuma Shobō.

Bates, D., Mächler, M., Bolker, B. & Walker, S. (2015). Fitting linear mixed-effects models using lme4. *Journal of Statistical Software*, 67(1), 1–48. https://doi.org/10.18637/jss.v067.i01

Carl, M. (2012a). A Computational Cognitive Model of Human Translation Processes. *Emerging Applications of Natural Language Processing: Concepts and New Research*, (110–128). https://doi.org/10.4018/978-1-4666-2169-5.CH005

Carl, M. (2012b). Translog - II: a Program for recording User Activity Data for empirical reading and writing research. *Proceedings of the Eight International Conference on Language Resources and Evaluation (LREC'12)*, 4108--4112. Istanbul: European Language Resources Association.

Carl, M. & Kay, M. (2011). Gazing and Typing Activities during Translation: A Comparative Study of Translation Units of Professional and Student Translators. *Meta*, 56(4), 952–975. https://doi.org/10.7202/1011262ar

Carl, M, Schaeffer, M., & Bangalore. S. (2016). The CRITT Translation Process Research Database. In Carl, M., S. Bangalore and M. Schaeffer (eds.), *New Directions in Empirical Translation Process Research: Exploring the CRITT TPR-DB*, pp. 13--54. Berlin: Springer. https://doi.org/10.1007/978-3-319-20358-4_2

Carl, M, & Schaeffer, M. (2017). Why translation is difficult: A corpus-based study of non-literality in post-editing and From-Scratch Translation. *HERMES - Journal of Language and Communication in Business* (56): 43--57. Aarhus: The School of Communication and Culture at Aarhus University. https://doi.org/10.7146/hjlcb.v0i56.97201

Hirose, Y. (2003). Recycling prosodic boundaries. *Journal of Psycholinguistic Research*, 32 (2): 162--195. https://doi.org/10.1023/A:1022448308035

Jakobsen, A., & Jensen, K. (2008). Eye movement behaviour across four different types of reading task. In Göpferich, S, A. Jakobsen & I. Mees (eds.) *Looking at Eyes: Eye-Tracking Studies of Reading and Translation Processing*. (Copenhagen Studies in Language 36), pp. 103--124. Copenhagen: Samfundslitteratur.

Kudo, T, Yamamoto, K., & Matsumoto, Y. (2004). Applying conditional random fields to Japanese morphological analysis. *Proceedings of the 2004 Conference on Empirical Methods in Natural Language Processing*, 230--237. https://aclanthology.org/W04-3230

Kuznetsova, A., Brockhoff, P. B., & Christensen, R. (2017). lmerTest Package: Tests in linear mixed effects models. *Journal of Statistical Software*, 82(13): 1--26. https://doi.org/10.18637/jss.v082.i13

Lacruz, I., Carl, M., & Yamada, M. (2018). Literality and cognitive effort: Japanese and Spanish. *Proceedings of the Eleventh International Conference on Language Resources and Evaluation (LREC 2018)*, 3818--3821. https://aclanthology.org/L18-1603

Lüdecke, D. (2021). sjPlot: Data Visualization for Statistics in Social Science (version 2.8.10). https://CRAN.R-project.org/package=sjPlot

Ruiz, C., Paredes, N., Macizo, P., & Bajo, M. (2008). Activation of lexical and syntactic target language properties in translation. *Acta Psychologica*, 128 (3): 490--500. https://doi.org/10.1016/j.actpsy.2007.08.004

Mizuno, A. (2005). Process Model for Simultaneous Interpreting and Working Memory. *Meta*, 50(2), 739–752. https://doi.org/10.7202/011015ar

Mizuno, A. (2022). *Junokuri no yaku to johokozo* [Linear translation and information structure] [Manuscript in preparation]. 97--130. Hituzi Syobo.

Naganuma, M., Funayama, C., Inou, K., Mizuno A., Ishizuka, H., & Tatsumi, A. (2016). *Sight translation kenkyu no kanosei* [The possibilities of sight-translation research]. *Invitation to Interpreting & Translation Studies*, 16, 142–162.

Nakamura, C., & Arai, M. (2012). *Nihongo garden-pathbun shori niokeru shobunseki heno keito to saibunseki no shorihuka* [The degree of commitment to the initial analysis predicts the cost of reanalysis: Evidence from Japanese garden-path sentences]. 2012 nendo nihon ninchi kagakukai dai 29 kai taikai happyo ronbunshu *[Proceedings of the 29th Annual Meeting of the Japanese Cognitive Science Society]*, Japan, 718–722. The Japanese Cognitive Science Society.

Ogawa, H. (2021). Difficulty in English-Japanese Translation: Cognitive Effort and Text/Translator Characteristics (Publication No. kent1627043401904391) [Doctoral dissertation, Kent State University]. OhioLINK Electronic Theses and Dissertations Center. http://rave.ohiolink.edu/etdc/view?acc_num=kent1627043401904391.

Okamura, Y., & Yamada, M. (2020). *Junokuri yaku no kihan to mohan: Dojituyaku wo mohan toshita kyoikuron nosiron* [On Junokuri yakuor Linear Translation Strategy]. *MITIS Journal*, 1(2), 25–48.

R Core Team. (2021). R: A Language and Environment for Statistical Computing. https://www.R-project.org/

Royer, J., Greene, B. A. & Sinatra B. M. (1987). The Sentence verification technique: A practical procedure for testing comprehension. Journal of Reading, 30 (5): 414--422. http://www.jstor.org/stable/40029713

Wickham, H. (2016). ggplot2: Elegant Graphics for Data Analysis. Springer-Verlag New York. https://doi.org/10.1007/978-0-387-98141-3

Yamada, M., & Naganuma, M. (2019). *Einichi sight translation no process ni kansuru yobiteki kosatsu* [A study on sight translation process between English and Japanese]. *Interpreting and Translation Studies*, 19, 97–113.

Proficiency and External Aides: Impact of Translation Brief and Search Conditions on Post-editing Quality

Longhui Zou lzou4@kent.edu
Michael Carl mcarl6@kent.edu
Kent State University, Ohio, USA

Masaru Yamada masaru.yamada@rikkyo.ac.jp
Takanori Mizowaki 22wv006d@rikkyo.ac.jp
Rikkyo University, Tokyo, Japan

Abstract

This study investigates the impact of translation briefs and search conditions on post-editing (PE) quality produced by participants with different levels of translation proficiency. We hired five Chinese student translators and seven Japanese professional translators to conduct full post-editing (FPE) and light post-editing (LPE), as described in the translation brief, while controlling two search conditions i.e., usage of a termbase (TB) and internet search (IS). Our results show that FPE versions of the final translations tend to have less errors than LPE versions. The FPE translation brief improves participants' performance on fluency as compared to LPE, whereas the search condition of TB helps to improve participants' performance on accuracy as compared to IS. Our findings also indicate that the occurrences of fluency errors produced by experienced translators (i.e., the Japanese participants) are more in line with the specifications addressed in translation briefs, whereas the occurrences of accuracy errors produced by inexperienced translators (i.e., our Chinese participants) depend more on the search conditions.

1 Introduction

Post-editing (PE) has become widely used in industrial translation. In some domains, more than 40% of translation practices are conducted as PE (JTF, 2020). However, PE does not mean that translators simply use machine translation (MT) to translate. In practice, MT systems must be integrated into an authentic environment, such as CAT tools, with which professional translators can perform PE operations including searches for terminology, concordance, usage of external resources on websites, etc. In addition, PE must often satisfy given quality requirements — as to whether it is full PE (FPE) or light PE (LPE) — which are normally described in the work instruction a translation brief. Thus, differences in search conditions — internet search (IS) or availability of termbase (TB) — and translation brief (i.e., LPE/FPE) may affect the translator's psychology and working style, which in turn may impact cognitive load during the translation process (effort) and the translation product (quality).

While the differences in the work environment and task conditions affect the process and product, few previous studies have taken this into account. There are possibly two reasons for it. The first reason is that an authentic translation environment capable of collecting translation process data was not previously available. For example, Translog-II, which is an experimental tool for researchers to collect translators' keyboard input and gaze data, does not provide the functionality that professional translators are used to in conventional CAT tools(Carl, 2012). The other reason has to do with translation conditions. The establishment of the international PE guidelines, ISO 18587 in 2017 has led to a certain common understanding with respect to what has to be post-edited. However, the industry definition of PE has not always been used which makes it difficult to compare the results of PE studies across the research. For example, it is often unclear whether a study focused on LPE or FPE.

Given this background, the purpose of this study is to have translators translate in an authentic translation work environment, collect translation process data, and compare and verify differences of translation performance. The term "authentic environment", in our definition, means 1) ensuring that PE is conducted in a professional CAT environment (Trados Studio in our case), as well as that translators are allowed to use IS or TB, and 2) providing appropriate work instructions that specify whether the task is FPE or LPE. The variable 1) is referred to as "search condition", and 2) is considered to be the "translation brief". In this way, this study examines differences in product-process interactions, considering these conditions (as variables) that will affect PE processes and products.

2 Literature review

There exist many comparative analyses of translation products and processes under different task conditions (from-scratch translation, PE) and work environments. However, to the best of our knowledge, no previous literature has directly examined the impact of differences in translation briefs (e.g., LPE vs. FPE) on PE quality.

A translation brief specifies the intended audience and purpose of the translation in the target language. Translation briefs are meant to bias (or prime) translators, to activate particular, but not other, "bodies of thought" (Gutt, 2004, p. 13) that answer to a specific translation expectations. Pym (2003, p. 486) points out that the notion of translation brief is "a key point in German-language Skopos theorie since 1984". For Nord (2006, p. 142) translation depends on the "conclusions the translator draws from the brief [...] it is no longer the source-text [alone] that guides the translator's decisions but the overall communicative purpose the target text is supposed to achieve in the target culture." Also Sturm (2017, p. 16) mentions that "Translation briefs and technical guidelines offer indications both about author intentions and the background of the target audience", and by now several translation companies offer guidelines that explain how to draft translation briefs [1].

Melby et al. (2012, p. 7) defines translation from a process-oriented perspective as follows: "Translation is the process of creating target language content that corresponds to the source content according to agreed-upon specifications". Melby's concern is the relationship of translation to the "specifications" or the required functions of the translation in the given context. This idea applies to PE tasks. Melby et al. (2014) argue that error-category-based specifications should be used to define quality in MTPE projects. The specification that Melby et al. promote is MQM (Multidimensional Quality Metrics), developed in the EU-funded QTLaunchPad project (Lommel et al., 2014).

Although the definition of FPE and LPE has been clarified with the development of ISO 18587, the international standard for PE (ISO, 2017), this definition is ambiguous for use in practice. Nunziatini and Marg (2020) provide clearer instructions and methods for post-editors, based on their own industry experience, by correlating instructions of FPE and LPE with MQM error typologies. In the same vein, (Sakamoto and Yamada, 2022) propose a risk management

[1] See https://toppandigital.com/us/blog-us/write-effective-translation-brief/, https://harryclarktranslation.co.nz/successful-translation-brief-made/.

method for which each translation task must include the client's requirements which should be broken down into issue typologies that are applied during PE with consideration of their severities.

Nitzke et al. (2019) have described this pre-production process from this risk management perspective. They claim that decision-making processes which include - among other things - the understanding of translation brief should be taught during the translation education. It is important, they say, to consider the constraints, conditions and expected translation quality for each task. This has been compiled as PE guidelines (Hu and Cadwell, 2016; Massardo et al., 2017) which stress that the translation brief has a significant impact on the translation process and product as well.

The following literature deals with interactions between different task conditions or "parameters" and differences in their performance.

Daems and Macken (2020) carried out an experiment with two groups of participants. One group were revisers who usually check/edit human translations. The other group consisted of post-editors who are used to correct MT output. In this experiment, the raw MT output and the human translations were given to both the revisers and the post-editors, but participants were not informed of the type of the texts given to them. The study compared the quality of the translations after each group's edit. The result shows that, the revisers outperformed the post-editors when they edited MT output. However, the post-editors outperformed the revisers when they edited human translations. While in every case accuracy errors remain intact, this outcome suggests that different conditions influence the performance of the revisers and post-editors.

In connection with this, "search conditions" are also important. For example, is the CAT tool available for the PE, is a glossary provided, and/or is plenty of time and pay given for external searches? Whether or not sufficient working conditions are prepared is a prerequisite for fulfilling the expected requirements.

Search conditions for external resources such as IS relevant to the subject matter in the course of translation are vital to the translator, and this will also affect translators' performance. Onishi and Yamada (2020) compared search behaviors of professional and novice translators. They found that professional translators devote a higher percentage of time and operations into searches. They found a high correlation between accuracy errors and the frequency and depth of searches. These findings suggest that IS during translation will greatly affect translators' quality.

3 Experimental design

In our study, we investigate how the two controlled parameters, i.e., translation brief and external search, interact with the participants' different levels of translation proficiency.

3.1 Participants

The PE experiment was conducted with two groups of participants using the same English source texts (STs) and Google neural machine translation (GNMT) outputs. One group comprises five Chinese translation students with simplified Chinese as their L1 and English as their L2. Seven Japanese professional translators with L1 in Japanese and L2 in English make up the other group. Participants were requested to fill out a questionnaire about their basic information before attending the experiment, which included language use on a daily basis, language learning experience, language proficiency, translation experience, PE experience, etc. Chinese participants had an average of 2.4 years of professional translation experience, whereas Japanese participants had an average of 7 years, as shown in the following Table 1. The twelve participants of both groups attended the experiment individually, using the same CAT tool, Trados

Studio, version 2019, without a time limit.

Years of experience	Minimum	Maximum	Mean	Standard deviation	Variance
Participant-ZH	0	6	2.4	2.24	5.04
Participant-JA	1	17	7.0	5.24	27.43

Table 1: Translation experience of participants

3.2 Materials

We selected four English source texts (STs) with general topics from previous American Translators Association (ATA) certification examinations. These exams were intended and considered to be a general professional-level assessment for translators (Koby and Champe, 2013). Among them, two texts were for English-to-Chinese ATA exams and two texts were for English-to-Japanese ATA exams. Each text is around 250 words long and contains about 10 segments. Their readability scores (Flesch-Kincaid Grade Level) are relatively similar, as shown in Table 2.

Text	Topic	Word count	Segment count	Readability score
1	Welfare	260	11	15.5
2	Tourism	242	12	12.3
3	War	263	11	13.9
4	Racism	257	13	15.2

Table 2: General descriptions of the four STs

We used GNMT to translate the four STs into simplified Chinese and Japanese and used this material to prepare four TMs for the Chinese participants and four TMs for the Japanese participants. We chose 28 words or phrases in the STs that had terminology errors in the GNMT outputs for any of the two language pairs (i.e., English-Chinese or English-Japanese) and generated a TB with the same set of English source terms and their equivalent Chinese and Japanese target terms.

3.3 Experimental layout

We provided two kinds of translation briefs to the participants: LPE (l) and FPE (f). We also controlled two conditions of external search for the PE experiment: i.e., TB provided within Trados interface but no access to other external resources (t), and access to any IS but no TB provided within Trados interface (s). Therefore, each participant conducted the PE of the four texts under four orthogonal tasks respectively, as illustrated in Table 3.

Brief/Condition	TB	IS
LPE	Plt	Pls
FPE	Pft	Pfs

Table 3: Four experimental tasks for each participant

For all the experimental tasks, the participants were presented with the GNMT outputs segment by segment appearing on the target text (TT) section as well as the TM section of the Trados interface in the same way as 100% matches with the TM. Under this experimental setup, we controlled that the participants of the same language pair had access to the same sets of GNMTs at a segment level. The working interface for the participants in the experiment is shown in Figure 1.

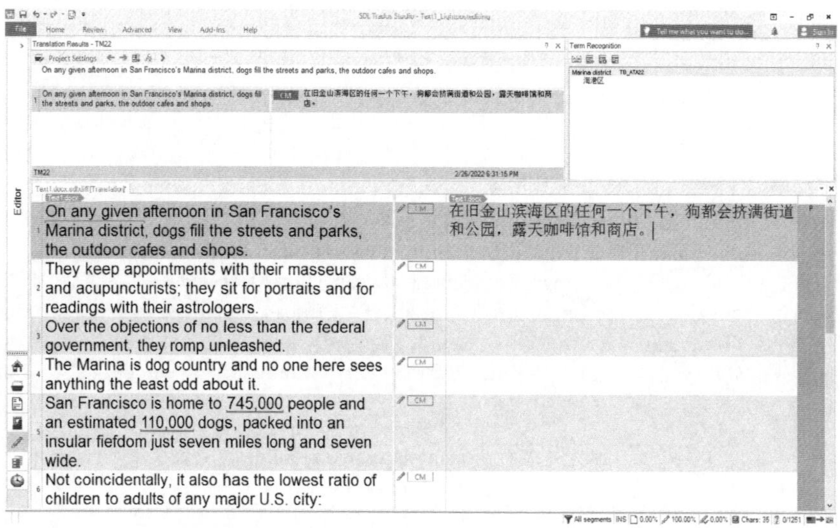

Figure 1: Working interface in Trados for the participants

Before their PE session started, each participant was given the translation briefs for the four texts with the descriptions of FPE and LPE defined by ISO 18587 (ISO, 2017), as shown in Appendix A. To ensure that the sequence of the tasks will not have an impact on our evaluation of the experiments, we randomized the experiment layout for each participant by permuting the four texts and keeping the succession of the four PE tasks in the same order.

For the TB condition, the participants were presented with the terminology appearing on the TB section of the Trados interface. Once there was one or several terms in an ST segment that they were working on match the terms in the TB that we prepared, the participants could check the TB on the upper right corner of the Trados workbench.

For the IS condition, the participants were presented with an empty TB appearing on the TB section of the Trados interface in the same way as 0% matches with TB. In this way, we assume that the participants were working in a near-authentic and familiar working environment of translation. The experimental layout is shown in Appendix B.

3.4 Data collection

The keystroke data during the PE sessions were recorded by both the Qualitivity plugin for Trados and eye tracker software (i.e., Tobii Studio 3.3.2 and Web Link). The translator's eye movement data were collected with the Tobii TX 300 eye tracker and the Eyelink 1000 plus for the EN-ZH and EN-JA experiments respectively. The translation process data (keystroke and gaze data with their production times) was then converted and processed by the newly launched research tool, Trados-Translog interface available at CRITT TPR-DB (Zou and Carl, 2022; Yamada et al., 2022). We found that the new tool can successfully be utilized to synchronize keystroke and gaze data from text production sessions into various data tables at different levels of granularity, including the text (SS), the segment (SG), the alignment group (AG), and translation unit (TU).

4 Quality assessment

Two professional translators (one Chinese and one Japanese) were hired to annotate the translation errors in the simplified Chinese and Japanese GNMT outputs as well as in the 12 PE versions. Because the STs of ATA exams are specifically designed to incorporate challenges that may result in translation errors associated with the categories and severity of errors under the grading framework of ATA, annotators in this experiment were given guidelines for error annotation based on an ATA-adapted annotation schema. [2]

Errors were divided into six types, "Mistranslation", "Usage", "Terminology", "Grammar", "Omission/Addition" and "Other". The former four types were further annotated as "Critical" and "Minor" errors depending on the severity of errors. As a result, there were altogether ten different kinds of errors, i.e., Mistranslation_Critical, Mistranslation_Minor, Usage_Critical, Usage_Minor, Terminology_Critical, Terminology_Minor, Grammar_Critical, Grammar_Minor, Omission/Addition, and Other.

In this experiment, the annotation was conducted on the level of AG. Annotators were asked to proceed in two steps: first, they should conduct word-level alignment between the TT and their corresponding ST. Then in the second step, AGs were assigned an error as applicable. When they came across an error that they considered an omission or addition, however, they were not required to do an alignment. In other words, there are only AGs for errors excluding "Omission/Addition" in this research.

For the purpose of this study, the occurrences of "Mistranslation", "Terminology", and "Omission/Addition" errors were grouped under the label of "Accuracy" error, while "Usage", "Grammar", and "Other" errors were grouped under the label of "Fluency" error. Additionally, all kinds of translation errors were grouped under the label of "Critical" and "Minor" Errors according to their annotated severity. Therefore, we gained four subcategories of errors under study, such as "Accuracy_Critical", "Accuracy_Minor", "Fluency_Critical", and "Fluency_Minor".[3]

5 Results

5.1 Error distribution

The twelve participants produced altogether 658 segments from the output of the two GNMT systems (i.e., simplified Chinese and Japanese). Because Omission errors only occur on the ST side, and Addition errors only occur on the TT side, we count both source and target words in an AG that involve each of the aforementioned four subcategoriess of errors (i.e., "Accuracy_Critical", "Accuracy_Minor", "Fluency_Critical", and "Fluency_Minor"). Since the STs for all the post-editors are identical, we can examine the total error counts for each of the four error subcategories in the raw GNMT output and the PEMT versions following the manual annotation by the two translators.

As illustrated in Figure 2, the error distribution of the GNMT has similar pattern as that of the PEMT. That is, the most frequent errors for GNMT and PEMT were, respectively, Fluency_Minor errors (50.59% and 46.86%), followed by Accuracy_Critical errors (22.93% and 30.92%), Accuracy_Minor (18.55% and 17.57%), and Fluency_Critical errors (7.93% and 4.65%). As these figures show, PEMT has lower percentages of fluency and critical accuracy errors than the GNMT. The results also show that fluency errors are usually minor errors, while accuracy errors are more often considered critical(Carl and Báez, 2019; Zou et al., 2021).

We also compare the raw total error counts for each experimental task, i.e., Pfs, Pft, Pls,

[2]See https://www.atanet.org/certification/how-the-exam-is-graded/error-categories/.

[3]In this research, "Omission/Addition" error were grouped under the label of "Critical" error, whereas "Other" error were grouped under the label of "Minor" Error.

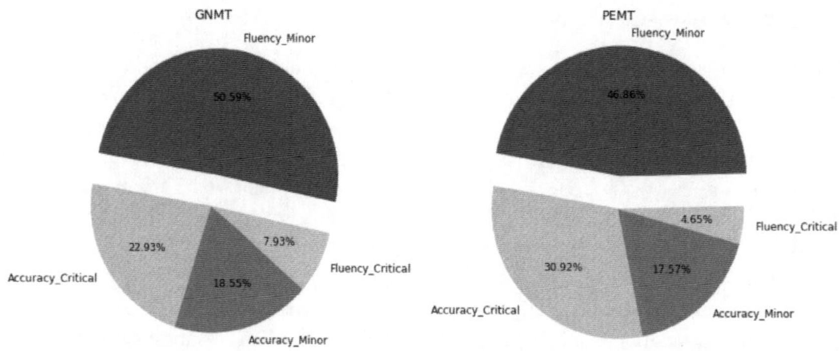

Figure 2: Error Distribution of GNMT and PEMT

Plt. The results in Figure 3 show that FPE versions have less total errors than LPE versions. Considering jointly all Japanese and Chinese versions, Pfs leads to less Fluency_Critical errors while Plt produces the most Fluency_Critical errors. Pft versions tend to have the least Fluency_Minor errors while Plt tend to have the most Fluency_Minor errors. Furthermore, Pft and Plt versions tend to have less Accuracy_Critical errors than the other two versions. Overall, compared to LPE, the translation brief of FPE improved the participants' performance on fluency, and - compared to IS - the provided TB improved the participants' performance on accuracy in our total data-set of experienced and less-experienced post-editors.

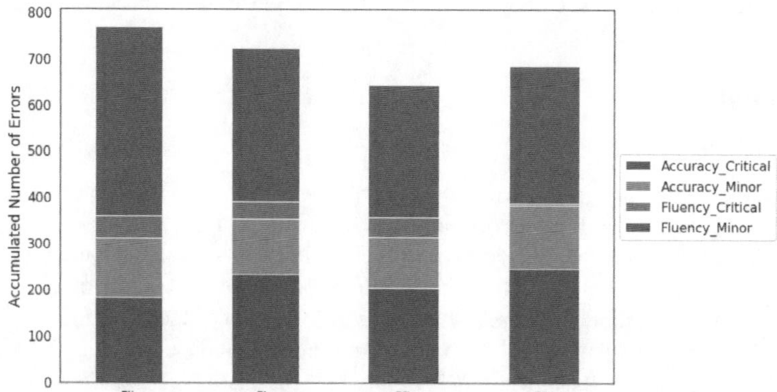

Figure 3: Error distribution across tasks

5.2 PE tasks

However, the focus of this study is to compare the effect of translation briefs (FPE or LPE) and search conditions (TB or IS) on PE quality between groups of participants with varying levels of translation proficiency. We use mixed two-way ANOVA with four dependent variables which correspond to the four error labels discussed above (i.e., Accuracy, Fluency, Critical, and Minor). The within-group independent variable consists of the four PE tasks (i.e., Plt, Pls, Pft and Pfs), and the between-group independent variable is the participant group, Chinese (zh) or Japanese (ja). Our findings indicate that across the four PE tasks, the PE versions of Chinese (novice) participants show significantly more Accuracy and Critical errors than Japanese (expert) participants. These results may be expected, as they confirm that more experienced (Japanese) translators consistently provide higher quality translations than less experienced (Chinese) ones (Shreve, 2006). While the Chinese novices produce in general more Accuracy and Critical errors, there is no significant interaction between the PE tasks and participant groups. In other words, the PE versions of Japanese participants have to the same extent less accuracy and critical errors than Chinese participants regardless of the PE tasks.

Across the four PE tasks, we also identify different tendencies of Accuracy and Fluency errors between the Chinese and Japanese groups of participants. As shown in Figure 4, there is no significant difference in Accuracy errors across all the four tasks for the Japanese participants. However, we observe that Accuracy errors fluctuate throughout the four tasks for the Chinese participants. While Chinese participants with the LPE translation brief (Plt and Pls) do not exhibit a discernible difference in Accuracy errors as compared to the FPE brief (Pft and Pfs), they tend to produce fewer Accuracy errors within the TB condition (Plt and Pft) as compared to the IS condition (Pls and Pfs). That is, they seem to be able to make better use of the TB than with free search (IS), but are largely indifferent to the translation brief.

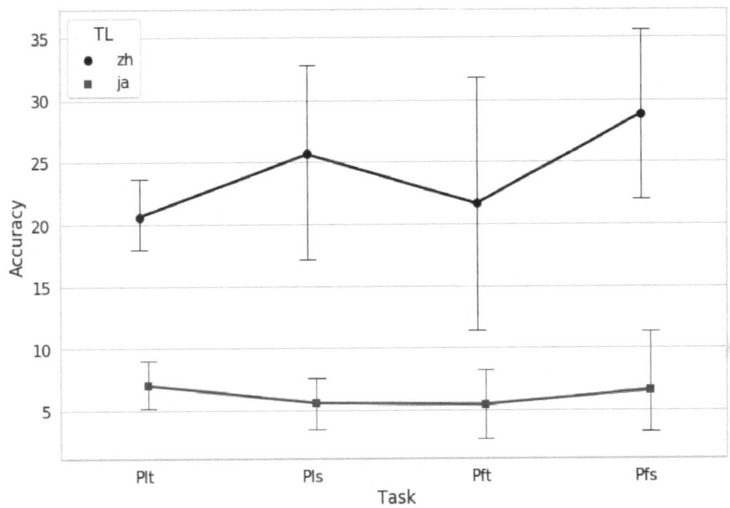

Figure 4: Comparing accuracy errors across tasks between Japanese and Chinese participants

On the other hand, we can clearly see a gradual decrease in Fluency errors for the Japanese participants when the PE task changes from LPE with TB (Plt) and LPE with IS (Pls), to FPE with TB (Pft) and FPE with IS (Pfs), as indicated in Figure 5. The PE versions of the Japanese participants have fewer Fluency errors with a FPE translation brief as opposed to LPE. Additionally, their PE versions show less Fluency errors under the IS condition as compared to TB. For the Chinese participants, however, their PE versions do not demonstrate stark differences in the occurrences of Fluency errors across the four tasks. As the LPE conditions asks to ignore Fluency issues in the MT output, this finding indicates to us that experienced (Japanese) translators are more sensitive to the translation brief than inexperienced (Chinese) translators. Surprisingly, we find that for Chinese participants, the PE versions of the FPE with TB (Pft) show more Fluency errors than the LPE with IS (Pls).

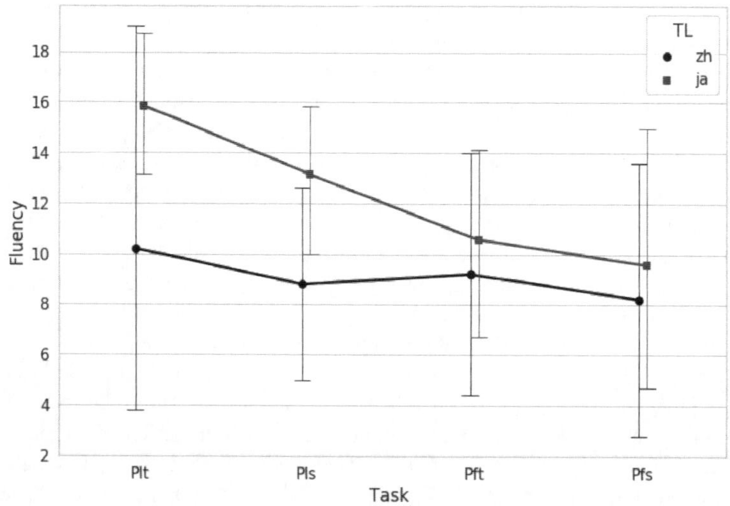

Figure 5: Comparing fluency errors across tasks between Japanese and Chinese participants

5.3 Translation proficiency

In the previous section, we investigate the difference between the two groups of participants regarding the impact of the four PE tasks. In this section, we further test if the impact of translation briefs and search conditions on PE quality are significantly different within each of the two groups of participants (Chinese and Japanese, respectively). We employ two-way ANOVA for each participant group, with four dependent variables which correspond to the four error labels (i.e., Accuracy, Fluency, Critical, and Minor). The two independent variables include translation brief (brief) and search condition (search). Our findings indicate that for Chinese participants, there are no statistically significant differences in the means of any error labels when comparing the translation briefs of FPE and LPE, but there are statistically significant differences in the mean of Accuracy errors between the TB and IS conditions ($p=.02<.05$), as shown in the following Table 4.

ANOVA Summary					
	df	sum_sq	mean_sq	F	PR(>F)
Brief	1.0	7.07	7.07	0.32	0.57
Search	1.0	119.98	119.98	5.41	0.02
Brief:Search	1.0	0.71	0.71	0.03	0.86
Residual	231.0	5119.41	22.16	NaN	NaN

Table 4: ANOVA summary for Accuracy errors of Chinese participants

On the other hand, when comparing the search conditions of TB and IS, there are no statistically significant differences in the means of any error labels for Japanese participants, but there are statistically significant differences in the mean of Fluency errors between the translation briefs of FPE and LPE, as illustrated in the following Table 5. However, for both groups of participants, the interaction between translation brief and search condition has no statistically significant impact on the frequency of any error labels.

In short, the Chinese participants are more sensitive to the control of the search conditions

ANOVA Summary					
	df	sum_sq	mean_sq	F	PR(>F)
Brief	1.0	96.60	96.60	6.34	0.01
Search	1.0	40.73	40.73	2.67	0.10
Brief:Search	1.0	13.93	13.93	0.91	0.34
Residual	324.0	4938.24	15.24	NaN	NaN

Table 5: ANOVA summary for Fluency errors of Japanese participants

relating the Accuracy errors out of the four error labels. Additionally, there is no significant difference when it comes to the control of translation briefs regarding all the error labels. The Japanese participants, on the other hand, are more sensitive to the control of translation briefs relating the Fluency errors. Additionally, there is no significant difference when it comes to the control of search conditions regarding all the error labels. We suppose this results from the disparity in translation competence between inexperienced and experienced translators. Since inexperienced translators, as illustrated by the Chinese participants in this study, tend to have less profession-related competence (e.g. research skills) than experienced translators, as illustrated by the Japanese participants in this study, their PE versions have significantly less Accuracy errors when they are using the prepared set of terminology than when they are asked to search online but without proper research capabilities. Furthermore, as experienced translators tend to have a greater awareness of the differences between various translation briefs than less experienced translators do, their PE versions typically contain less Fluency errors when they are required to perform FPE rather than LPE. This is because experienced translators have more pragmatic competence than less experienced translators do (e.g., functional knowledge linked to translation briefs) (Yang and Li, 2021).

6 Conclusion

This paper aims to investigate the impact of translation briefs (full PE, FPE vs. light PE, LPE) and search conditions (provided termbase TB vs. free internet search IS) on PE quality of two groups of participants with varying levels of translation proficiency. To this purpose, four English STs from previous ATA certification exams (47 sentences, about 1,000 words) were automatically translated into simplified Chinese (zh) and Japanese (ja) by google NMT (GNMT), and were post-edited by five Chinese student translators and seven Japanese professional translators, respectively. The study was thus carried out in two language pairs (en-zh, en-ja) and the 12 post-editors produced a total of 658 segments. Keystrokes were logged and gaze data recorded, but these aspects of the experiment are not addressed in this paper.

To run the experiment under ecologically valid working conditions of professional translators, we conducted the experiment in the Trados workbench using the new Trados-Translog interface (Zou and Carl, 2022; Yamada et al., 2022). We asked participants to post-edit four texts under two types of translation briefs, i.e., FPE (f) and LPE (l), and two types of search conditions, i.e., TB (t) and IS (s). Therefore, we had four different PE tasks for each participant, i.e., Pfs, Pft, Pls, Plt.

The Chinese and Japanese GNMT outputs and the corresponding post-edited versions were annotated for translation errors based on an ATA-adapted error taxonomy. We grouped the errors under four labels, i.e., "Accuracy", "Fluency", "Critical", and "Minor" errors. We calculated the error count by segment, aggregated them over the four PE tasks, and compared the error distribution in the two raw GNMT outputs (simplified Chinese and Japanese) and in the twelve post-edited versions. Our results show a similar error distribution for GNMT output and the PEMT versions. For both, GNMT and PEMT, minor fluency and critical accuracy errors were more common than other subcategories of errors. PEMT has generally lower percentages of fluency and minor errors than the GNMT, but a higher percentages of critical accuracy errors.

Looking into the error distribution for each of the tasks we see that, overall, FPE versions tend to have less errors than LPE versions. The translation brief of FPE improves in particular the participants' performance on fluency as compared to LPE, and the provided TB seems to improves the participants' performance on accuracy as compared to IS.

Across the four PE tasks, there are notable more Accuracy and Critical errors for Chinese than for Japanese participants. These results are to be expected, to the extent that the more experienced Japanese translators ought to deliver more frequently translations of higher quality than our inexperienced Chinese translators. Our findings also shows that inexperienced translators have significantly fewer accuracy errors in the TB condition as compared to searching online (IS). We assume that this is the case since less experienced translators typically possess less research skills (PACTE, 2003, 2005; Göpferich et al., 2009).

Experienced translators, on the other hand, seem to better realize implications of the translation briefs: with respect to accuracy errors, there is no significant difference across the four PE tasks. However, in the FPE condition, experienced translators produce less fluency errors as compared to LPE condition. This difference has not been observed for the less experienced translators, which suggests that experience leads to more awareness of the variations between different translation briefs.

Due to the restrictions of accessibility to the translators of our experimental language pairs, we only recruited twelve participants for this study. Therefore, there are certain limitations in the statistical results due to the relatively small sample size. However, we are currently collecting more data and intend to look into other aspects of translation process and translator behavior in future studies. The datasets are publicly available in the TPR-DB (Carl et al., 2016) and the reported results replicable.

References

Carl, M. (2012). Translog-ii: A program for recording user activity data for empirical reading and writing research. In *Proceedings of the Eighth International Conference on Language Resources and Evaluation (LREC'12)*, pages 4108–4112.

Carl, M. and Báez, M. C. T. (2019). Machine translation errors and the translation process: a study across different languages. *Journal of Specialised Translation*, 31:107–132.

Carl, M., Schaeffer, M., and Bangalore, S. (2016). The critt translation process research database. In *New directions in empirical translation process research*, pages 13–54. Springer.

Daems, J. and Macken, L. (2020). Post-editing human translations and revising machine translations: Impact on efficiency and quality. In *Translation Revision and Post-Editing*, pages 50–70. Routledge.

Göpferich, S., Jakobsen, A. L., and Mees, I. M. (2009). *Behind the mind: Methods, models and results in translation process research*, volume 37. Samfundslitteratur.

Gutt, E.-A. (2004). Applications of relevance theory to translation-a concise overview. *Retrieved March*, 4:2009.

Hu, K. and Cadwell, P. (2016). A comparative study of post-editing guidelines. *Baltic Journal of Modern Computing*, 4(2):346–353.

ISO (2017). *ISO 18587: Translation Services: Post-editing of Machine Translation Output: Requirements*. ISO.

JTF (2020). *2020 Nendo Honyaku Tsuyaku Hakusho: Dai 6 Kai Honyaku-Tsuyaku Gyokai Chosa Houkokusho [JTF Translation and Interpreting Report 2020: The 6th TI industry white paper]*. Japan Translation Federation.

Koby, G. S. and Champe, G. G. (2013). Welcome to the real world: Professional-level translator certification. *Translation & Interpreting, The*, 5(1):156–173.

Lommel, A., Uszkoreit, H., and Burchardt, A. (2014). Multidimensional quality metrics (mqm): A framework for declaring and describing translation quality metrics. *Revista Tradumàtica: tecnologies de la traducció*, 12:455–463.

Massardo, I., van der Meer, J., O'Brien, S., Hollowood, F., Aranberri, N., and Drescher, K. (2017). Taus mt post-editing guidelines.

Melby, A., Fields, P., Hague, D. R., Koby, G. S., and Lommel, A. (2014). Defining the landscape of translation. *Tradumàtica*, 12:0392–403.

Melby, A. K., Housley, J., Fields, P. J., and Tuioti, E. (2012). Reliably assessing the quality of post-edited translation based on formalized structured translation specifications. In *Workshop on Post-Editing Technology and Practice*.

Nitzke, J., Hansen-Schirra, S., and Canfora, C. (2019). Risk management and post-editing competence. *The Journal of Specialised Translation*, 31:239–259.

Nord, C. (2006). Translating as a purposeful activity: a prospective approach. *Teflin Journal*, 17(2):131–143.

Nunziatini, M. and Marg, L. (2020). Machine translation post-editing levels: Breaking away from the tradition and delivering a tailored service. In *Proceedings of the 22nd Annual Conference of the European Association for Machine Translation*, pages 309–318.

Onishi, N. and Yamada, M. (2020). Why translator competence in information searching matters: An empirical investigation into differences in searching behavior between professionals and novice translators. *Invitation to Interpreting and Translation Studies*, 22:1–22.

PACTE (2003). Building a translation competence model. *Triangulating translation: perspectives in process oriented research. Amsterdam;*.

PACTE (2005). Investigating translation competence: Conceptual and methodological issues. *Meta*, 50(2):609–619.

Pym, A. (2003). Redefining translation competence in an electronic age. in defence of a minimalist approach. *Meta: journal des traducteurs/Meta: Translators' Journal*, 48(4):481–497.

Sakamoto, A. and Yamada, M. (forthcoming, 2022). Managing clients' expectations for mtpe services through a metalanguage of translation specifications: Mppqn method. In *Metalanguages for Dissecting Translation Processes:Theoretical Development and Practical Applications*, pages 191–199. Routledge.

Shreve, G. M. (2006). The deliberate practice: translation and expertise. *Journal of translation studies*, 9(1):27–42.

Sturm, A. (2017). Metaminds: Using metarepresentation to model minds in translation. *Empirical modelling of translation and interpreting*, 7:419.

Yamada, M., Mizowaki, T., Zou, L., and Carl, M. (2022). Trados-to-translog-II: Adding gaze and qualitivity data to the CRITT TPR-DB. In *Proceedings of the 23rd Annual Conference of the European Association for Machine Translation*, pages 293–294, Ghent, Belgium. European Association for Machine Translation.

Yang, Z. and Li, D. (2021). Translation competence revisited: Toward a pedagogical model of translation competence. *Advances in Cognitive Translation Studies*, pages 109–138.

Zou, L. and Carl, M. (2022). Trados and the critt tpr-db: Translation process research in an ecologically valid environment. In *Model building in empirical translation studies: Proceedings of TRICKLET Conference, May 19-20, 2022*, pages 38–40.

Zou, L., Carl, M., Mirzapour, M., Jacquenet, H., and Vieira, L. N. (2021). Ai-based syntactic complexity metrics and sight interpreting performance. In *International Conference on Intelligent Human Computer Interaction*, pages 534–547. Springer.

Appendices

A Translation brief

A.1 Full post-editing

On this level of post-editing, the output shall be accurate, comprehensible and stylistically adequate, with correct syntax, grammar and punctuation. The aim of this level of post-editing is to produce an output which is indistinguishable from human translation output. Nevertheless, it is recommended that post-editors use as much of the MT output as possible. On this level of post-editing, post-editors shall focus on:

a) ensuring that no information has been added or omitted;

b) editing any inappropriate content;

c) restructuring sentences in the case of incorrect or unclear meaning;

d) producing grammatically, syntactically and semantically correct target language content;

e) applying spelling, punctuation and hyphenation rules;

f) ensuring that the style appropriate for the text type is used and that stylistic guidelines provided by the client are observed;

g) applying formatting rules.

A.2 Light post-editing

Light post-editing is normally used when the final text is not intended for publication and is mainly needed for information gisting, i.e. for rendering the main idea or point of the text. In this level of post-editing, the output shall be comprehensible and accurate but need not be stylistically adequate. At this pot-editing output level, post-editors should focus on:

a) using as much of the raw MT output as possible;

b) ensuring that no information has been added or omitted;

c) editing any inappropriate content;

d) restructuring sentences in the case of incorrect or unclear meaning.

B Experimental layout of the PE tasks

Proband	Task 1	Task 2	Task 3	Task 4
P01	Plt1	Pls2	Pft3	Pfs4
P02	Plt2	Pls3	Pft4	Pfs1
P03	Plt3	Pls4	Pft1	Pfs2
P04	Plt4	Pls1	Pft2	Pfs3
etc.				

Table 6: Experimental layout of the PE tasks

Note: The tasks for P05 are the repetition of the tasks for P01, and the tasks for P06 are the repetitions of P02, etc.

Entropy as a measurement of cognitive load in translation

Yuxiang Wei yuxiang.wei3@mail.dcu.ie
Centre for Translation and Textual Studies, Dublin City University, Ireland

Abstract

In view of the "predictive turn" in translation studies, empirical investigations of the translation process have shown increasing interest in studying features of the text which can predict translation efficiency and effort, especially using large-scale experimental data and rigorous statistical means. In this regard, a novel metric based on entropy (i.e., HTra) has been proposed and experimentally studied as a predictor variable. On the one hand, empirical studies show that HTra as a *product*-based metric can predict effort, and on the other, some conceptual analyses have provided theoretical justifications of entropy or entropy reduction as a description of translation from a *process* perspective. This paper continues the investigation of entropy, conceptually examining two ways of quantifying cognitive load, namely, shift of resource allocation and reduction of entropy, and argues that the former is represented by surprisal and ITra while the latter is represented by HTra. Both can be approximated via corpus-based means and used as potential predictors of effort. Empirical analyses were also conducted comparing the two metrics (i.e., HTra and ITra) in terms of their prediction of effort, which showed that ITra is a stronger predictor for TT production time while HTra is a stronger predictor for ST reading time. It is hoped that this would contribute to the exploration of dependable, theoretically justifiable means of predicting the effort involved in translation.

1. Introduction

In recent years, process-oriented translation studies which investigate the "black box" of the translator's mind have been prolific and less of a speculative nature, due to the emergence of new methodologies for collecting, processing, and analysing behavioural data. While early research depends heavily on think-aloud protocol, more recent ones tend to adopt relatively sophisticated techniques including eye tracking, electroencephalography (EEG), functional magnetic resonance imaging (fMRI), etc. Such experimental tools have largely enabled translation process research (TPR) to become increasingly predictive (Schaeffer et al., 2019). Large-scale, multilingual, and comparable behavioural data collected via these tools (e.g., the CRITT TPR-DB; see Carl, Schaeffer et al., 2016), and analysed through rigorous statistical approaches, have provided a necessary means for building models of human translation "which makes specific, falsifiable predictions regarding the process and the product of translation" (Carl, Bangalore et al., 2016, p. 4). This allows for systematic investigations beyond the *description* of translation, taking a step further towards *explaining*, and especially *predicting*, translation phenomena from empirical observations.[1]

[1] When Holmes (1972) argued for an independent academic status for translation studies, it was described as an empirical discipline in nature, where there are two main objectives of inquiry: "(1) to describe the phenomena of translating and translation(s) as they manifest themselves in the world of our experience, and (2) to establish general principles by means of which these phenomena can be explained and predicted." (Quoted from the republished version of Holmes' paper in Venuti, 2000, p. 176)

Not surprisingly, it has been argued that a "predictive turn" is now being triggered in translation studies, constituting a new paradigm where predictive methods and models, driven by large-scale empirical data, are adapted to the cognitive processes of translation (Schaeffer et al., 2019).

This is the result of two aspects of technological development, namely, the machine learning approaches to translation (e.g., Neural Machine Translation) and the computational techniques that facilitate the empirical modelling of the human translation process (ibid). For the latter, the fact that many aspects of behaviour and cognition have become increasingly measurable and quantifiable (e.g., translators' strategies, typical translation patterns, and cognitive effort), and the use of rigorous statistical and computational tools, seem to have made it possible "for the first time to empirically model the translation process" (ibid, p. 5).

1.1 Entropy as a predictor variable

In view of this predictive turn, there has been increasing interest in investigating, especially by statistical means, particular features of the text that can predict the efficiency and cognitive load/effort [2] of translation, post-editing, interpreting, and other modes of translation production. These studies examine the translation product in relation to those aspects of the process which can be used as measurements of translation efficiency or difficulty. For example, eye-key span has been shown to be predicted by the number of translation alternatives for the ST word in question (Dragsted, 2010; Dragsted and Hansen, 2008), and reading time can be predicted by the change of word order between the ST and TT, the number of occurrences of the word in previous context, the length of phrases, etc. (Jensen et al., 2009)

Another novel metric which has been recently proposed and empirically examined is word translation entropy (see, e.g., Carl, Schaeffer, et al., 2016 p. 29-33). This entropy-based predictor variable, often denoted as HTra, is typically considered a statistical measure of the translation product which represents variance, literality, and translation ambiguity (Carl, 2021b; Carl, Bangalore, et al., 2016), and is used in many empirical investigations to analyse its correlation with effort, to find evidence for early priming processes, and to discuss ways of quantifying translation difficulty. It has also been considered a better measure for the variation of the translation alternatives than simply counting the number of these alternatives (Bangalore et al., 2016). Further studies on word translation entropy show a positive and statistically significant effect on different measures of effort, including, among others, first fixation duration, word production duration, the probability of a fixation, and total reading time (e.g., Carl and Schaeffer, 2017; Schaeffer et al., 2016). In other words, HTra predicts effort. On the basis of such empirical findings, words with higher HTra values have often been considered more difficult to translate (Carl et al., 2019).

1.2 Entropy as a mental process

For such and many other studies, the concept of entropy seems to be consistently used as a measure of the *product*, rather than as a representation of specific aspects of mental states during the process, nor as a way of describing the process of transition between one mental

---

[2] Although the terms "cognitive load" and "cognitive effort" can sometimes be confusing and are often used interchangeably, this paper considers cognitive *load* as the difficulty that is posed by a task or process (i.e., the required amount of cognitive effort), and considers cognitive *effort* as the actual effort expended in the process or task, where this effort is realised by optimising the allocation of limited cognitive resources.

state and another. An exception, however, is the "systems theory perspective" (Carl et al., 2019), where the human translation process is considered "a hierarchy of interacting word and phrase translations systems which organize and integrate as dissipative structures" (p. 211), and where entropy is defined as the internal order of these word translation systems. Expenditure of cognitive effort to arrive at a translation solution — where this effort is described as "average energy" (ibid) — decreases the internal entropy (i.e., disorder) of the system. In this regard, the definition of entropy is apparently from a systems theory perspective.

In terms of the conceptual investigations of entropy in relation to the mental states, Wei (2021) analyses translation entropy from a different perspective, focussing more on the probabilistic nature of this concept (as Kullback-Leibler divergence, see Kullback, 1959), the dynamic change of probability distribution, the uncertainty of choice, its representation of cognitive resource allocation in the activation, suppression, competition, and selection of candidates when multiple options are available (i.e., when the ST is translation-ambiguous), and the specific processes in which entropy is reduced through the transition of mental states. The process of lexical translation selection is analysed in close detail through the lens of entropy and entropy reduction. This brings the concept into the assumed mental states, using entropy to describe and explain cognitive activities when mental states transition between one another during lexical activation and selection. Following these conceptual explorations, Wei's (2021) study also examines the behavioural manifestations of this process through detailed observation of eye movements in a large database (i.e., the CRITT TPR-DB).

In Wei's (2021) analyses, the mental processes in translation are conceptualised under the assumption of non-selective co-activation of both source and target languages, similar to most studies that draw inferences from bilingualism. Upon encounter of a particular ST item, possible translations for this item would be subliminally co-activated, and the translator is assumed to "engage in an activation pattern where the activated items receive different degrees of priority for resource allocation" (p. 170). This pattern would then be dynamically updated during lexical selection, where there is continual shift of cognitive resource allocation as mental states transition from one towards another. The shift of resource allocation results in reduction of entropy and expenditure of cognitive effort. In this view, the amount of cognitive effort needed in the process (i.e., the cognitive load imposed) can thus be quantified via two means — either the shift of cognitive resource allocation, or the reduction of entropy (ibid).

The present paper examines these two ways of quantification, and argues that the shift of resource allocation can be represented by surprisal of the item selected (i.e., ITra, see below), and that the reduction of entropy can be represented by HTra (as formulated in Carl, Schaeffer, et al., 2016).

Section 2 briefly reviews the concept of surprisal, focusing on its conceptualisation as a means of quantifying cognitive load in psycholinguistics. This lays the foundation for the discussion on relative entropy in the subsequent section 3, where surprisal (also described as ITra in recent studies) will be shown to be equivalent to the *relative entropy* between the final and initial mental states of the translation choice. This means that the required amount of cognitive effort in the transition between these mental states can be determined by surprisal (ITra), if one adopts the formulation in resource-allocation processing difficulty.

Section 4 demonstrates that if one adopts another means for quantifying effort (i.e., reduction of entropy value), this effort would be represented by HTra.

Section 5 provides further discussion on HTra and ITra, leading to an empirical investigation in Section 6 where the two metrics are compared in terms of their prediction of translation effort. Section 7 ends the paper with concluding remarks.

2. Surprisal and ITra

In psycholinguistics, surprisal (i.e., negative logarithm of probability) is often used as an important quantification of cognitive load (Attneave, 1959; Hale, 2001; Levy, 2008, 2013; Levy and Gibson, 2013), especially in the context of structural disambiguation. The surprisal of a word in its context is considered a useful quantification of the cognitive effort required to process this word during online sentence processing (see Hale, 2001). This is because, from that view, incremental sentence comprehension is a step-by-step disconfirmation of possible phrase-structural analyses for the sentence, which means that cognitive load can be interpreted as the combined difficulty of disconfirming the disconfirmable structures at a particular point of the sentence (i.e., at a given word).

This quantification of cognitive load also raises "a unified treatment of structural ambiguity resolution and prediction-derived processing benefits" (Levy, 2013 p. 158). Both Hale (2001) and Levy (2008) illustrate much successful use of the surprisal framework for explaining a variety of psycholinguistic phenomena, many of which are closely relevant to garden-path sentences (i.e., temporary ambiguity). In addition, theoretical justifications for surprisal as a metric for cognitive processing difficulty has not been lacking (see e.g., Levy, 2013), especially within the frameworks of rational cognitive models (Shepard, 1987; Tenenbaum and Griffiths, 2001). Difficulty, or measurable disruption, in real-time sentence processing can arise either from an overload in memory (i.e., an overload in the cognitive resources for the storage and retrieval of the representational units which are used to analyse the linguistic input), or from a sufficiently unexpected input which causes a shift in cognitive resource allocation "to various alternatives in the face of uncertainty" (Levy, 2013 p. 144). Although theories based on the former (i.e., resource-limitation theories) have been a dominant paradigm for studies of differential processing difficulty, the latter (i.e., resource-allocation approach) has been a line of investigation which largely has ambiguity resolution as a primary concern (Levy, 2008).

In the latter approach (i.e., resource-allocation), the *size* of the shift in cognitive resource allocation which is induced by a word is indicative of the difficulty in processing this word, and the size of this shift is equivalent to the *change* (i.e., update) in the conditional probability distribution over all interpretations before and after the word (Levy, 2013). Mathematically, this change would be measured in terms of entropy (e.g., Cover and Thomas, 1991) — specifically, the *relative entropy* of the conditional distributions before and after encountering the word.

This seems largely consistent with the use of word translation entropy to measure the difficulty of a translation choice in the face of uncertainty (at the lexical, rather than syntactic, level), where this difficulty can be represented by the conditional probability distribution over TT alternatives.

Of particular note is that in sentence comprehension, the *relative entropy* mentioned above has been shown to be equivalent to the *surprisal* of the word in question (Levy, 2008 pp. 1131-1132), which Levy views as the reranking cost in incremental disambiguation where cognitive resources are re-allocated to the possible analyses of the sentence.

Here, it is worth mention that the concept of *surprisal* is also known — in different contexts — as information, self-information, or Shannon information content, all referring to essentially the same mathematical equation (i.e., the negative logarithm of probability). In some recent papers, the surprisal regarding a particular translation item is specifically called *word translation information*, and denoted by ITra (see e.g., Carl, 2021a; Heilmann and Llorca-Bofí, 2021). These terms, although focusing on quite different aspects, are in fact mathematically expressed in the same manner as the surprisal discussed here (i.e., the negative logarithm of probability, or equivalently, the logarithm of the inverse of the probability).

3. ITra and relative entropy

As mentioned in 1.3, the cognitive effort that is required in the word translation selection process (i.e., the cognitive load imposed by this process) is proposed to be quantifiable by either the shift in resource allocation, or the reduction of entropy (see Wei, 2021 for details). The size of the shift in cognitive resource allocation would be represented mathematically by relative entropy (i.e., Kullback-Leibler convergence), whereas the reduction entropy would simply be the absolute difference of entropy values, regarding the initial and final stages of the process.

In other words, there are two ways of representing cognitive load via entropy — relative entropy and decrease of entropy. Here, the relative entropy of the mental state at the end of the process, with respect to the initial stage of activation, will be shown below as being equal to the surprisal (i.e., ITra) of the TT item eventually chosen by the translator.

At the end of the selection process (i.e., when the mental processing has arrived at a decision as to which particular target item is to be selected), the distribution of cognitive resources in the mental state can be reasonably assumed to have, after a series of continual update (or shift) which incurs cognitive effort, eventually concentrated on one single item (i.e., the item chosen by the translator) whose probability therefore equals 1 given this mental state. According to the definition of Kullback-Leibler divergence (i.e., relative entropy), the divergence of the updated distribution $Q(\mathrm{x})$ from the original distribution $P(\mathrm{x})$ equals the expectation of the logarithmic difference between $Q(\mathrm{x})$ and $P(\mathrm{x})$, with the expectation taken using $Q(\mathrm{x})$. Suppose there are n possible items in the mental lexicon (i.e., n values for x in $\mathrm{x} \in \chi$), among which the item chosen by the translator is W, then the above description would mean that $Q(W)=1$, that $Q(\mathrm{x})=0$ when $\mathrm{x} \neq W$, and that $P(\mathrm{x})$ represents the probabilities in the initial activation pattern for both $\mathrm{x}=W$ and $\mathrm{x} \neq W$. In this case, the divergence $D_{KL}(Q \parallel P)$ would be:

$$D_{KL}(Q \parallel P) = \sum_{x \in \chi} Q(x) \log\left(\frac{Q(x)}{P(x)}\right)$$

$$= \sum_{i=1}^{n} Q(x_i) \log\left(\frac{Q(x_i)}{P(x_i)}\right)$$

$$= Q(W) \log\left(\frac{Q(W)}{P(W)}\right) + (n-1) \lim_{Q(x) \to 0^+} Q(x) \log\left(\frac{Q(x)}{P(x)}\right)$$

$$= \log \frac{1}{P(W)} + (n-1) \lim_{Q(x) \to 0^+} Q(x) \log\left(\frac{Q(x)}{P(x)}\right)$$

$$= -\log P(W) + (n-1) \lim_{Q(x) \to 0^+} Q(x) \log\left(\frac{Q(x)}{P(x)}\right)$$

$$= -\log P(W) + (n-1) \lim_{Q(x) \to 0^+} [\, Q(x) \log Q(x) - Q(x) \log P(x) \,]$$

$$= -\log P(W) + (n-1) [\, \lim_{Q(x) \to 0^+} Q(x) \log Q(x) - \lim_{Q(x) \to 0^+} Q(x) \log P(x) \,]$$

As $\lim_{Q(x) \to 0^+} Q(x) \log P(x) = 0$ and

$$\begin{aligned}
\lim_{Q(x)\to 0^+} Q(x)\log Q(x) &= \lim_{Q(x)\to 0^+} \frac{\log Q(x)}{\frac{1}{Q(x)}} \\
&= \lim_{Q(x)\to 0^+} \frac{\frac{d}{d(Q(x))}\log Q(x)}{\frac{d}{d(Q(x))}\frac{1}{Q(x)}} \\
&= \lim_{Q(x)\to 0^+} \frac{\frac{1}{Q(x)\ln 10}}{-\frac{1}{[Q(x)]^2}} \\
&= -\lim_{Q(x)\to 0^+} \frac{Q(x)}{\ln 10} \\
&= 0
\end{aligned},$$

it then follows that

$$D_{KL}(Q \parallel P) = -\log P(W)$$

In other words, the Kullback-Leibler divergence of these two distributions (i.e., the relative entropy between initial activation and final selection) equals the surprisal of the item that is eventually chosen by the translator, i.e., $-\log P(W)$.

As the $P(W)$ in the surprisal equation here represents the probability of W in the initial activation pattern (i.e., when W is first activated together with all other items), this surprisal should in theory refer to the surprisal in the corresponding mental state at the initial stage, rather than the surprisal of the item in the textual material.

However, if the activation of lexical items is modulated by context and the frequency of the different meanings/translations (e.g., in the re-ordered access model, see, e.g., Duffy et al., 2001), the $P(x)$ which describes the mental state of activation would be the same as the probabilities that can be observed in the text. This means that the initial surprisal for this item W in the mental state, i.e., $-\log P(W)$, can be approximated by, if not equivalent to, its surprisal in the text.

In this manner, the relative entropy with respect to the above mental process would be, albeit arguably, equal to the corresponding surprisal in the text. Cognitive load can thus be represented by this surprisal (consistent with Levy's formulation), and in turn approximated by corpus-based analyses. As mentioned in Section 2, this surprisal is the same as word translation information (ITra).[3]

4. HTra and decrease of entropy

Similarly, the initial entropy value in the mental state would be equal to the entropy value that is observed in the text (i.e., HTra). If the *decrease* of entropy value, i.e., the absolute difference between the two respective entropy values regarding the initial and final mental states, is used as a measurement of cognitive effort in the selection process, then at the point when the translation choice is made, this decrease would equal the initial entropy when all the

[3] It is important to note that the CRITT TPR-DB estimates this value on the basis of the translation choices made by all participants in each experiment. However, the surprisal here can in fact be approximated in other ways as well, using different corpus data, and would result in different ITra values than those in the CRITT TPR-DB. This is the same for HTra.

TT candidates are activated given the ST item (i.e., the entropy in the mental state between activation and selection), and in turn equal the HTra value. This will be shown below in detail.

Specifically, when the choice is made, the entropy in the mental state refers to the entropy for distribution Q(x), which equals zero:

$$H_1(x) = -\sum_{x \in \mathcal{X}} Q(x) \log Q(x)$$

$$= -\sum_{i=1}^{n} Q(x_i) \log Q(x_i)$$

$$= -Q(W) \log Q(W) - (n-1) \lim_{Q(x) \to 0^+} Q(x) \log Q(x)$$

$$= -Q(W) \log Q(W)$$

$$= 0$$

The initial entropy associated with the pattern of activated lexical items, i.e., the entropy in the initial mental state, is as follows:

$$H_0(x) = -\sum_{x \in \mathcal{X}} P(x) \log P(x) = -\sum_{i=1}^{n} P(x_i) \log P(x_i)$$

where $P(x_i)$ refers to the conditional probability with which x_i is to be selected, given the mental state at the initial stage of activation.

Accordingly, the decrease of entropy between these two points, i.e., from P(x) to Q(x), or from initial activation to final selection, would be simply:

$$H(x) = H_0(x) - H_1(x) = H_0(x) = -\sum_{i=1}^{n} P(x_i) \log P(x_i)$$

Here, if the activation of lexical items is modulated by context and the frequency of meanings/translations, as mentioned in Section 3, the P(x) in this equation can be considered equal to the probabilities observed in the text. This means that the H(x) here would be the same as the entropy equation which is formulated in Carl et al. (2016), i.e., that which is calculated from the probabilities in the text and approximated from the sample. In other words, the decrease of entropy value in the mental state is perhaps equal to the HTra value.[4]

5. HTra and ITra

The above sections have shown that between the two ways of quantifying cognitive load in lexical translation choice, namely, shift of resource allocation and reduction of entropy (see Wei, 2021), the former is equal to surprisal of the chosen item and the latter is equal to the entropy generalising over all alternative options. Both can be approximated from the text (as ITra and HTra), and can perhaps be used as theoretically justifiable ways of quantifying cognitive load. This means that these two formulations can provide useful means for predicting the effort of translation at the lexical level.

[4] See previous footnote.

So two metrics, HTra and ITra, merit further discussion. If they are considered from a *product* perspective, the difference between them seems straightforward — HTra generalises over different translation items while ITra indicates the unpredictability of a specific translation item given a particular ST token (see also Carl, 2021a, p. 122; Heilmann & Llorca-Bofí, 2021, pp. 213-214). From a *process* perspective, the above sections have shown that between the mental state of initial activation and that of final selection, HTra represents the reduction of entropy while ITra indicates the size of the shift in cognitive resource allocation.

In terms of their mathematical expression, HTra represents the initial $P(x)$ distribution when alternative options are activated, whereas ITra indicates the surprisal of the final choice. HTra is equivalent to the *absolute difference* of entropy between the two mental states, while ITra is equivalent to the *relative* entropy of the final mental state with respect to the initial mental state.

In this regard, it is worth asking — which metric is a better predictor of translation behaviour, if we examine the empirical data? To answer this, a few smaller questions need to be addressed: Does HTra still predict effort if we control for the effects of ITra, and vice versa? If so, which one has a larger strength of prediction? When HTra is controlled, does ITra make an additional contribution in explaining variance in effort (and vice versa)?

6. Prediction of effort

A subset of the CRITT TPR-DB[5] was used to examine these two predictors (i.e., HTra and ITra) in terms of their significance and strength in predicting production time and ST/TT reading time. This data is within the multiLing dataset, where six English texts are translated into various languages. In total, the data used for analysis includes 500 experimental sessions from six studies (AR19, BML12, ENJA15, KTHJ08, RUC17, and ST12).

Production time is represented by Dur and refers to the duration of TT production for each ST token. For reading time, early measures of eye movement include first fixation duration on the ST token (FFDur), first pass duration on the ST token (FPDurS), and first pass duration on the TT token (FPDurT). Late measures are total reading time on the ST (TrtS) as well as on the TT (TrtT). All these were regarded as response variables in the analysis and examined in relation to HTra and ITra.

For each of these response variables, outliers were removed by 2.5 standard deviations per participant, and a sequential multiple regression analysis was conducted. In the regression analysis of each response variable, HTra was first entered as a predictor, then ITra is added. A comparison between the base model (with HTra only) and the full model (with both HTra and ITra) can show the contribution of ITra in explaining the variance in the response variables.

A set of base models with ITra entered was also examined in relation to the full model, shedding light on the contribution of HTra in explaining the variance in production time and reading time.

Through an examination of the full models in greater detail, the strength and significance of each predictor (HTra and ITra), when controlling for the other predictor, was also analysed.[6]

[5] This is a publicly available database. For details, see, e.g., Carl, Bangalore, et al. (2016). A description of the up-to-date public studies is also available on the CRITT@kent website: https://sites.google.com/site/centretranslationinnovation/tpr-db/public-studies?authuser=0

[6] VIF scores in the full models are all between 1.9 and 2.1.

6.1 Production time (Dur)

For the prediction of word production time, results are shown in Tables 1 and 2.

The two base models (Dur 1 and Dur 2), for HTra and ITra respectively, are both significant. For HTra, $R^2 = .03$, $F(1, 30104) = 957.42$, $p < .001$, and the model explained 3% of the variance in production time. For ITra, $R^2 = .05$, $F(1, 30314) = 1453.19$, $p < .001$. Here, the model with ITra explained a higher percentage (5%) of the variance than that with HTra.

The full model where both predictor variables were entered (Dur 3) was also significant, $R^2 = .05$, $F(2, 30103) = 748.75$, $p < .001$. With the two predictors combined, this model explained 5% of the variance in production time.

Here, although the impact of both ITra and HTra was strong and significant in the full model, it is apparent that ITra ($\beta = 689.58$) was more than three times as a stronger predictor than HTra ($\beta = 196.05$).

After controlling ITra, adding HTra to the base model did not lead to any R^2 change (see Dur 2 and Dur 3). This means that with ITra controlled, no additional variance was explained by HTra. In contrast, when ITra was added after controlling HTra, the model significantly explained an additional 2% of the variance (see Dur 1 and Dur 3). In other words, while controlling for the other predictor variable, ITra made an additional contribution in explaining the variance in production time, whereas HTra did not.

	Dur 1	Dur 2	Dur 3
(Intercept)	2434.25 ***	2434.25 ***	2434.25 ***
HTra	675.76 ***		196.05 ***
ITra		825.96 ***	689.58 ***
N	30106	30106	30106
R2	0.03	0.05	0.05

All continuous predictors are mean-centered and scaled by 1 standard deviation.
*** p < 0.001; ** p < 0.01; * p < 0.05.

Table1. Prediction of production time (Dur)

6.2 ST Reading time (FFDur, FPDurS, TrtS)

Table 2 illustrates the results for the prediction of FFDur, FPDurS, and TrtS. Similar to the results for production time, all impacts in all models here were significant, for all measures of ST reading time. However, for both early and late measures of eye movement on the ST, HTra seemed to be a much stronger predictor than ITra, in contrast to the results for production time (see Section 6.1).

This is notable for all response variables regarding ST reading, where, for FFDur, HTra ($\beta = 45.75$) was more than three times as a strong predictor as ITra ($\beta = 13.03$), and for FPDurS, HTra ($\beta = 42.76$) was more than four times as strong as ITra ($\beta = 9.49$). For the late measure of eye movement on the ST (TrtS), HTra ($\beta = 222.22$) was twice as strong as ITra ($\beta = 103.51$).

For early measures (FFDur & FPDurS), HTra explained an additional 1% of the variance only in FPDurS. For late measures, no additional variance was explained by either variable.

	FFDur 1	FFDur 2	FFDur 3	FPDurS 1	FPDurS 2	FPDurS 3	TrtS 1	TrtS 2	TrtS 3
(Intercept)	188.54 ***	188.54 ***	188.54 ***	180.72 ***	180.72 ***	180.72 ***	960.87 ***	960.87 ***	960.87 ***
HTra	55.10 ***		45.75 ***	49.57 ***		42.76 ***	296.33 ***		222.22 ***
ITra		45.84 ***	13.03 ***		40.15 ***	9.49 ***		262.61 ***	103.51 ***
N	69191	69191	69191	69364	69364	69364	69256	69256	69256
R2	0.01	0.01	0.01	0.04	0.03	0.04	0.03	0.03	0.03

All continuous predictors are mean-centered and scaled by 1 standard deviation.
*** $p < 0.001$; ** $p < 0.01$; * $p < 0.05$.

Table 2. Prediction of ST reading time

6.3 TT Reading time (FPDurT, TrtT)

For both early and late measures of eye movement on the TT, HTra and ITra did not show a large difference in their strength of prediction, at least not as large as the difference shown above regarding ST reading (see Section 6.2), although all predictions are significant. These results are shown in Table 3.

	FPDurT 1	FPDurT 2	FPDurT 3	TrtT 1	TrtT 2	TrtT 3
(Intercept)	468.76 ***	468.76 ***	468.76 ***	2317.80 ***	2317.80 ***	2317.80 ***
HTra	195.00 ***		125.58 ***	706.94 ***		490.14 ***
ITra		186.87 ***	96.94 ***		653.80 ***	302.30 ***
N	68795	68795	68795	69025	69025	69025
R2	0.07	0.07	0.08	0.03	0.03	0.04

All continuous predictors are mean-centered and scaled by 1 standard deviation.
*** $p < 0.001$; ** $p < 0.01$; * $p < 0.05$.

Table 3. Prediction of TT reading time

7. Concluding remarks

The above sections have analysed, both theoretically and empirically, two ways of quantifying cognitive load in translation choice, namely, shift of resource allocation and reduction of entropy. Both can be approximated via corpus-based means. At a conceptual level, the paper argues that HTra approximates the reduction of entropy in the mental state and that ITra approximates the size of shift in cognitive resource allocation, providing theoretical justifications for both HTra and ITra as potential means of quantifying cognitive load. Empirical analyses on the CRITT TPR-DB showed that although both metrics had significant and strong impact on effort, ITra was a much stronger predictor for word production time while HTra was a stronger predictor for ST reading time. The difference between the two for prediction of TT reading was found to be relatively small. It is hoped that this would contribute to the search for a dependable means of predicting effort in translation.

References

Attneave, Fred. (1959). *Applications of Information Theory to Psychology: A Summary of Basic Concepts, Methods, and Results*. Oxford, England: Henry Holt.

Bangalore, Srinivas, Bergljot Behrens, Michael Carl, Maheshwar Ghankot, Arndt Heilmann, Jean Nitzke, . . . Annegret Sturm. (2016). Syntactic variance and priming effects in translation. In Michael Carl, Srinivas Bangalore, and Moritz Schaeffer (Eds.), *New Directions in Empirical Translation Process Research* (pp. 211-238). Cham, Switzerland: Springer.

Carl, Michael. (2021a). Information and entropy measures of rendered literal translation. In Michael Carl (Ed.), *Explorations in Empirical Translation Process Research* (pp. 113-140). Cham, Switzerland: Springer.

Carl, Michael (Ed.) (2021b). *Explorations in Empirical Translation Process Research*. Cham, Switzerland: Springer.

Carl, Michael, Srinivas Bangalore, and Moritz Schaeffer (Eds.). (2016). *New Directions in Empirical Translation Process Research: Exploring the CRITT TPR-DB*. Cham: Springer.

Carl, Michael, and Moritz Schaeffer. (2017). Why translation is difficult: A corpus-based study of non-literality in post-editing and from-scratch translation. *HERMES-Journal of Language and Communication in Business*(56), 43-57.

Carl, Michael, Moritz Schaeffer, and Srinivas Bangalore. (2016). The CRITT translation process research database. In Michael Carl, Srinivas Bangalore, and Moritz Schaeffer (Eds.), *New Directions in Empirical Translation Process Research* (pp. 13-54). Cham, Switzerland: Springer.

Carl, Michael, Andrew Tonge, and Isabel Lacruz. (2019). A systems theory perspective on the translation process. *Translation, Cognition & Behavior, 2*(2), 211-232. doi:10.1075/tcb.00026.car

Cover, Thomas M, and Joy A Thomas. (1991). *Elements of information theory*. New York: John Wiley & Sons.

Dragsted, Barbara. (2010). Coordination of reading and writing processes in translation. *Translation and Cognition, 15*, 41.

Dragsted, Barbara, and Inge Gorm Hansen. (2008). Comprehension and production in translation: a pilot study on segmentation and the coordination of reading and writing processes. *Copenhagen Studies in Language*(36), 9-29.

Hale, John. (2001, June). *A probabilistic Earley parser as a psycholinguistic model.* Paper presented at the Second Meeting of the North American Chapter of the Association for Computational Linguistics on Language technologies, Pittsburgh, Pennsylvania, 1- 7 June 2001. Association for Computational Linguistics.

Heilmann, Arndt, and Carme Llorca-Bofí. (2021). Analyzing the effects of lexical cognates on translation properties: A multivariate product and process based approach. In Michael Carl (Ed.), *Explorations in Empirical Translation Process Research* (pp. 203-229). Cham, Switzerland: Springer.

Holmes, James S. (1972). *The Name and Nature of Translation Studies*. Paper presented at the Translation Section of the Third International Congress of Applied Linguistics, Copenhagen.

Jensen, Kristian Tangsgaard Hvelplund, Annette C Sjørup, and Laura Winther Balling. (2009). Effects of L1 syntax on L2 translation. *Methodology, Technology and Innovation in Translation Process Research. Copenhagen: Samfundslitteratur*, 319-338.

Kullback, S. (1959). *Information Theory and Statistics*. Hoboken, NJ: John Wiley & Sons.

Levy, Roger. (2008). Expectation-based syntactic comprehension. *Cognition, 106*(3), 1126-1177.

Levy, Roger. (2013). Memory and surprisal in human sentence comprehension. In Roger van Gompel (Ed.), *Sentence Processing* (pp. 90-126). London and New York: Psychology Press.

Levy, Roger, and Edward Gibson. (2013). Surprisal, the PDC, and the primary locus of processing difficulty in relative clauses. *Front Psychol, 4*, 229. doi:10.3389/fpsyg.2013.00229

Schaeffer, Moritz, Barbara Dragsted, Kristian Tangsgaard Hvelplund, Laura Winther Balling, and Michael Carl. (2016). Word translation entropy: Evidence of early target language activation during reading for translation. In Michael Carl, Srinivas Bangalore, and Moritz Schaeffer (Eds.), *New Directions in Empirical Translation Process Research: Exploring the CRITT TPR-DB* (pp. 183-210). Cham, Switzerland: Springer.

Schaeffer, Moritz, Jean Nitzke, and Silvia Hansen-Schirra. (2019). Predictive turn in translation studies: Review and prospects. In Stanley Brunn and Roland Kehrein (Eds.), *Handbook of the Changing World Language Map*. Cham, Switzerland: Springer.

Shepard, Roger N. (1987). Toward a universal law of generalization for psychological science. *Science, 237*(4820), 1317-1323.

Tenenbaum, Joshua B, and Thomas L Griffiths. (2001). Generalization, similarity, and Bayesian inference. *Behavioral and Brain Sciences, 24*(4), 629-640.

Venuti, Lawrence (Ed.) (2000). *The Translation Studies Reader*. London: Routledge.

Wei, Yuxiang. (2021). Entropy and eye movement: A micro-analysis of information processing in activity units during the translation process. In Michael Carl (Ed.), *Explorations in Empirical Translation Process Research* (pp. 165-202). Cham, Switzerland: Springer.

Association for Computational Linguistics
209 N. Eighth Street
Stroudsburg, Pennsylvania 18360

ISBN 978-1-7138-6760-9

CURRAN ASSOCIATES INC.
proceedings.com